# Beautiful Shells

H. G. Adams, Groombridge and Sons

BIBLIOLIFE

# BEAUTIFUL SHELLS

THEIR

## Nature, Structure, & Uses Familiarly Explained

WITH

DIRECTIONS FOR COLLECTING, CLEANING, AND ARRANGING
THEM IN THE CABINET

AND DESCRIPTIONS OF

## THE MOST REMARKABLE SPECIES.

BY H. G. ADAMS,

*Author of "Nests and Eggs of Familiar Birds," "Beautiful Butterflies,"*
*"Humming Birds," "Favourite Song Birds," etc., etc.*

Illustrated.

LONDON:
GROOMBRIDGE AND SONS.

# CONTENTS.

## UNIVALVES.

CONTENTS.

# BIVALVES.

# MULTIVALVES.

———

# BEAUTIFUL SHELLS.

———◆———

## WHAT ARE SHELLS?

Dr. Johnson gives us no less than eight different meanings for the word Shell. First, he calls it "The hard covering of anything; the external crust." Second, "The covering of a testaceous or crustaceous animal." And here we may stop, for this is just the signification which has to do with our subject; so let us turn the sentence inside out, and see what we can make of it. We all know what a covering is—an outer coat, a case, a protection from injury, a husk, a crust, a—in short, a shell,—*scyll* or *scell*, as our Saxon forefathers called it; *schale*, as the Germans now term it. No Latin nor Greek here, but the good old Saxon tongue, somewhat rough and rugged, perhaps, but stout and sturdy, and honest and serviceable; a kind of language to stand wear and tear, like a pair of hobnailed shoes, with little polish, but useful, yes, very useful! Well, we have got so far, now comes a hard word—TES-TA-CE-OUS, what can it mean? It is pronounced *tes-ta-shus,* comes from the Latin *testaceus*—having a shell, and means consisting of, or composed of shells; so we find that a *testacean* is a shell-fish, and *testaceology* is the science of shells. Johnson's second meaning of the word *testaceous* is "Having continuous, not jointed shells, opposed to crustaceous." So we find that some naturalists call those testaceous fish, " whose strong and thick shells are entire and of a piece, because those which are joined, as the lobsters, are crustaceous."

Now some of the true testaceans have shells in more than one or two pieces, and therefore this last explanation of the term is rather calculated to mislead a learner; but we shall explain presently wherein the difference consists between them, and the CRUS-TA-CEOUS, or, as we pronounce it, *krus-ta-shus,* fish consists. Here is another long word, it comes from the Latin *crusta,* a word of many meanings, all having reference to an outer coat or covering. My readers know all about pie-crust, and have perhaps heard a surly, snappish, peevish person called a crusty fellow; they will now understand what is meant by a *crustacean* and *crustaceology*, that part of Zoology which treats of crustaceous animals. They constitute quite a large family, these *ologies*, and have a strange way of twisting themselves about, and exchanging limbs and features, so that one is puzzled at times to tell which is which. But here we have fixed two of them, called TESTACEOLOGY and CRUSTACEOLOGY, twin brothers, and very much alike in their characteristics. Let us have a good look at them, so that we may know them again if we should lose sight of them for awhile. Now we will spell over the name of the first—

## CONCHOLOGY.

Why, it is changed already! Has this science of shells then another name? Yes, and this is it, pronounced *kong-kol-o-gy*, and derived from the Latin *concha*, which means properly a shell-fish with two shells, joined by a hinge, as the oyster, the cockle, etc. This present volume then is a work on *Conchology*, the subject of it is *Conchiferous*, and whoever studies it will be doing something towards becoming a *Conchologist*.

## Beautiful Shells.

So much for names and titles ; but still we have the question to answer, What are shells? In a learned work called a Cyclopædia, we find it stated that " shell is the hard calcareous (that is chalky) substance which protects, either partially or entirely, the testaceous mollusks externally, or supports certain of them internally." All this you will understand, except perhaps the word " mollusks " ; this is a term applied to soft-bodied animals, such as shell-fish, snails, etc., about which we shall have more to say as we proceed. By this we learn that *all* shells are not external or outer coverings, some are internal or inner supports for the soft jelly-like bodies to which they belong, thus performing the duty of bones. An example of this is seen in the shell of the Cuttle-Fish, called by naturalists *Sepia,* a description of which will be found further on in the book.

Shells are either *Crystalline* or *Granular.* Now look at those two words, they almost explain their own meaning. Crystalline shells are those which have more or less of clearness, transparency as we say, so that if held against the light it shows through them ; they are sometimes called *Porcellaneous* shells, from their resemblance in this respect to porcelain, or chinaware; the Common

Cowry (*Cyprœa Tigris*) is a shell of this description.

*Granular,* or, as they are sometimes called, *Concretionary* shells, are the most hard and compact; it is in these that the substance called *nacre*, or *mother-of-pearl*, is mostly found. One of the commonest examples is the oyster shell; if broken across it will be seen to consist of very thin plates, or *laminæ*, as they are termed, closely packed together. The thinner these laminæ may be, the more lustrous and beautiful appears the lining of the shell; that shifting play of colours which we call *iridescent*, from *iris*, the rainbow, is then brightest and most noticeable. A very remarkable substance is this mother-of-pearl; smooth, and shining, and delicately-tinted. Who would expect to find such a beautiful lining to the rugged, rough, dingy-looking oyster, or mussel shell? Truly these mollusks, some of them, live in gorgeous palaces. And the most curious part of the matter is that from the fluids or juices of their own bodies, and from the chalky matter collected from the water, they are enabled to secrete or deposit such wonderfully-constructed habitations, which after all are little more than chalk. Burn a heap of oyster shells, or any other testaceous coverings, and you

get lime the same as that produced by burning the
white lumps from the chalk-pit, which lumps, by
the way, are said to be composed wholly, or for the
most part, of marine shells.  This we should call
*cretaceous* matter, from *creta,* which is the Latin for
chalk, or *calcerous,* from *calcis*—lime.  Granular
shells you have been told are sometimes called
*concretionary,* this is because they contain a large
amount of this chalky deposit.  The rock called
limestone, geologists tell us, is composed entirely
of fossil shells and mud, or what was once mud,
dried and hardened, most likely by extreme heat,
to the consistence of rock.  Wonderful this to
think of; huge mountains, and mighty masses, and
far-stretching strata, forming a large portion of the
crust of the earth, made up chiefly of the coverings
of fishes, a great portion of them so small as to be
scarcely visible to the naked eye.—Truly wonderful!
But we shall have more to say upon this head when
we come to speak of Fossil Shells, as well as on
the subject of Pearls, in our chapter on the fish in
whose shells they are chiefly found.

It has been a matter of dispute with naturalists whether the testaceous mollusks have shells
at all before they issue from the egg, and the main
evidence favours the opinion that, generally speak-

ing, they do possess what may be considered as
a kind of pattern or model of the habitation which
they are to build. This appears to be of a pale
horn-colour, and destitute of any markings; but as
soon as the animal enters upon an independent
state of existence, it begins to assume its distinctive
shape and colour, gradually increasing with the
growth of its living tenant, and becoming more
and more decidedly marked, until it attains its full
perfection of testacean development. Thus the age
of some shell-fish can be at once determined by the
peculiar conformation and markings of the shell.

The relative portions of animal and earthy, or
rather chalky matter, which compose these shells,
vary considerably in different kinds; in those
called Crystalline or Porcellaneous, the animal
deposit is much less than in the granular or concretionary shells, where it not only constitutes a
large part of the whole substance, but is more
dense, that is, thick, and also has the appearance
of being membranous, or organized matter. We
can perhaps best explain this by saying that whereas
the different chalky layers of the crystalline shell
seem merely glued together by the intervening
animal fluid; those of the granular shell, as the
oyster, appear to be connected by interlacing mem-

brancs. But all this my readers will learn more about from more advanced and scientific works if they proceed, as I trust they will do, in the study of CONCHOLOGY, a science which has in a greater or less degree attracted the attention of curious and contemplative minds in all ages, and the study of which it has been well said is peculiarly adapted to recreate the senses, and insensibly to lead us to the contemplation of the glory of God in creation.

## BEAUTY AND VALUE OF SHELLS.

In shells, as in all the works of the Almighty Creator, we may observe an infinite variety of form, and if they do not all strike us as alike graceful, yet in each, however plain and simple, there is some peculiar beauty, whether it be the mere hollow cup, or the simple tube, the smooth or twisted cone, the slender spire, the convoluted oval, or half circle, ribbed or spiked, with a lip curving out like the leaf of a water lily, or a narrow rim, like that of a golden chalice; they are indeed elegant, each perfect of its kind, and bearing the impress of a constructive skill far above that of man, who copies from them some of the most graceful and elegant designs wherewith to ornament his buildings, and shapes in which to fashion his articles of luxury or utility.

The most beautiful scroll-work of marble chimney-pieces, cornices of rooms, and other enriched portions of both public and private structures, are those in which the forms of shells have been taken for the patterns of the artistic designs; and how tasteful and appropriate is the employment of the shells themselves as ornaments for the mantel-piece, sideboard, and chiffonnier. Then, too—

> " The rainbow-tinted shell, which lies
> Miles deep at bottom of the sea, hath all
> Colours of skies, and flowers, and gems, and plants."

Not only has it grace and elegance of form, but it has also richness, and delicacy, and variety of colouring. In some species the tints are intensely vivid as the shifting lights of the aurora borealis, or the glowing hues of an autumnal sunset; in others pale and delicate as the first indications of coming morn, or the scarcely perceptible tinge of a just-expanding flower-bud; in some the colours are arranged in patterns, regularly disposed; in others, in masses and blotches, of varying shapes and degrees of intensity; in some again they seem to change and melt one into the other, like the prismatic hues of the rainbow. In all, whether distinct and unconnected, or intimately blended, whether regular or irregular, they are beautiful exceedingly. Nor is their beauty of an evanescent, that is, fading, or vanishing character; unlike plants and animals, which, when once dead, are extremely difficult of preservation, Shells, being composed of particles already in natural combination, are almost indestructible; unless exposed to the action of fire, or some powerful acid, they will remain the same for ages, requiring no care or attention, beyond occasionally removing the dust, which would collect upon and defile their pearly whiteness, or obscure the brilliancy of their colours.

So easily collected, arranged, and preserved, and withal so singular and graceful in form, and rich and various of tint, one cannot wonder that Shells have always had a conspicuous place in all museums, and other collections of natural history objects; neither can we feel surprised that a high value should have been set upon rare specimens; as much as a thousand pounds, it is said, has been given for the first discovered specimen of the *Venus Dione;* another shell, called the *Conus cedo nulli,* is valued at three hundred pounds; and the *Turbo scaloris,* if large and perfect, is worth one hundred

guineas; while the *Cypræa aurantium,* or Orange
Cowry, if it has not a hole beaten through it, will
fetch fifty guineas. It has been calculated that a
complete collection of British Conchology is worth
its weight in silver.

The following quotation is from " The Young
Conchologist," by Miss Roberts. Our readers will
do well to peruse it attentively :—" We admit that
shells are beautiful, and that they are admirably
adapted to the exigencies of the wearers ; but how
shall we account for the endless diversity of shades
and colours, varying from the sober coating of the
garden snail to the delicate and glowing tints which
are diffused over some of the finer species, in the
infinite profusion of undulations, clouds, and spots,
bands and reticulated figures, with which these
admirable architects enrich the walls of their
beautiful receptacles. The means of producing
them must be sought for in the animals themselves.
Their necks are furnished with pores replete with
colouring fluid, which blends insensibly with the
calcareous exudation already noticed, and thus
occasions that exquisite variety in their testaceous
coverings, which art attempts to emulate, but can
never fully equal. Thus far is the result of observation and experiment. It now remains to account

for the extraordinary fact that the stony exudations of testaceous animals condense only on those parts where they are essential to their welfare. But here investigation ends—the microscope has done its office. It seems as if material nature delighted to baffle the wisdom of her sons, and to say to the proud assertors of the sufficiency of human reason for comprehending the mysteries of creation and of Providence, thus far you can go, and no farther; even in the formation of a shell, or its insignificant inhabitant, your arrogant pretensions are completely humbled.'"

## USES OF SHELLS.

In speaking of shells as ornaments, and objects worthy of our study and admiration, we have already mentioned some of their uses, for surely that which contributes to the intellectual improvement and innocent pleasure of mankind, is in its degree useful. But on the more narrow ground of utility, shells may also claim a high place in our estimation. To man in a barbarous and uncivilized state, they furnish the means of performing some of the most important operations of daily life, being extensively used as a substitute for iron. The savage frequently forms his knife, his hunting spear, and his fish-hook

of hard shell. Lister relates that the inhabitants
of Nicaragua, in South America, fasten a shell,
called the *Ostrea virginica*, to a handle of wood, and
use it as a spade. In North America the natives
use a blue and white belt composed of shells, called
the *Venus mercenaria*, as a symbol of peace and
unity, and there, too, the gorget of the chieftain's
war-dress is composed of the pearl-bearing mussel,
called by naturalists *Mytilus margaritiferus*. Many
African tribes use the *Murex tritonis* as a military
horn, and a rare variety of this shell, which has the
volutions reversed, is held sacred, and used only by
the priests. Among the Friendly Islanders the
Orange Cowry is a symbol of the highest dignity.
The Money Cowry (*Cyprœa moneta*) forms the current coin of many nations of Africa; and a certain
number of these shells strung together, are considered by the slave-hunting chiefs as an equivalent
for so many black-skinned brothers, whom they sell
into hopeless bondage.

Among nations, too, in a high state of civiliza-
tion, shells are often used for economical, as well as
ornamental purposes. To say nothing of mother-
of-pearl, which is converted into so many articles,
useful as well as pretty, scallop, or oyster shells,
are frequently employed as scoops by druggists,

2

grocers, and the like; and in the country the dairy-maid, with the larger kinds of the same shell, skims her milk, and slices her butter; while sometimes by the poor people of both towns and villages, the deeper specimens are converted into oil-lamps. One very important use, my young readers will understand, when I speak of a ragged urchin, who shouts to every passer-by—" Please remember the grotto!"

In ancient times, we are told, the people of Athens recorded their votes on public occasions, by marks upon a shell, thus Pope says—

> " He whom ungrateful Athens would expel,
>   At all times just, but when he signed the shell;"

in allusion to this custom, of which we are reminded by such English words as *Attestation,* a certifying, a bearing witness; *Testify,* to give evidence; *Testament,* a will, or written disposal of property, etc.; all having their origin, it appears, in the Latin *testa*—a shell. In ancient poetry, we find the word *Testudo* used to signify a musical instrument, also called a lyre or lute; which instrument, according to tradition, was first made by passing strings, and straining them tightly, over the shell of a tortoise. So the poet Dryden, describing those who listened to the music drawn from this simple invention, says—

"Less than a God they thought there could not dwell,
    Within the hollow of that shell
        That spoke so sweetly."

A Greek writer, called Apollodorus, gives this account of the invention of music by the Egyptian god Hermes, more commonly known as Mercury. The Nile having overflowed its banks, and laid under water the whole country of Egypt, left, when it returned to its usual boundaries, various dead animals on the land; among the rest was a tortoise, the flesh of which being dried and wasted by the sun, nothing remained within the shell except nerves and cartilages, or thin gristly bones; these being shrunk and tightened by the heat, became sonorous, that is sounding. Against this shell Mercury chanced to strike his foot, and pleased by the sound caused thereby, examined the shell from which it came, and so got a notion, as we say, how he might construct a musical instrument. The first which he made was in the form of a tortoise, and strung with the dried sinews of dead animals, even as are the lutes, harps, and fiddles of our day. This fanciful mode of accounting for the origin of music is thus alluded to by a writer named Brown:

" The lute was first devised
In imitation of a tortoise' back,
Whose sinews parched by Apollo's beams,
Echoed about the concave of the shell;     [sound
And seeing the shortest and smallest gave shrillest
They found out frets, whose sweet diversity
Well touched by the skilful learned fingers,
Roused so strange a multitude of chords.
And the opinion many do confirm,
Because *testudo* signifies a lute."

And now we are among the myths and fables
of antiquity, we may just mention another applica-
tion of the shell to musical purposes.   Neptune,
who, according to the Grecian mythology, was the
god of the sea, is frequently represented as going
forth in his car in great state and pomp, with a
body-guard of Tritons; some of whom go before
with twisted conch shells as trumpets, with which
we are to suppose they make delightful harmony.
Venus, too, the goddess of beauty, rode on the
ocean foam in a testaceous car.   Thus Dryden says,
that Albion—our native land, so called on account
of its chalky cliffs, from the Latin *alba*—white,

" Was to Neptune recommended;
Peace and plenty spread the sails;
Venus in her shell before him,
From the sands in safety bore him."

But without believing all these fables, more poetical than true, we may soon convince ourselves that in the hollow chambers of a shell, there does seem to dwell, like an imprisoned spirit, a low, sad kind of music. An English poet, named Walter Savage Landor, has well described this in these lines—

> "Of pearly hue
> Within, and they that lustre have imbibed,
> In the sun's palace porch, where, when unyoked,
> His chariot wheel stands midway in the wave;
> Shake one, and it awakens; then apply
> Its polished lips to your attentive car,
> And it remembers its august abodes,
> And murmurs as the ocean murmurs there."

Wordsworth, too, gives a beautiful description of a child applying one of these pearly musical-boxes to his ear.

Many other uses of shells might be mentioned, to show that they perform an important part in the operations of nature, as the means and modes by and in which God sees fit to order the affairs of this world are frequently called; and also promote the ends of science, and the arts of every-day life. By the decomposition of the shells, of which they are partly composed, solid rocks frequently crumble to pieces, and spreading over a considerable surface, form a fruitful soil for the nourishment of vegetation. The character of the testaceous deposits, too, enable geologists (as those who study the nature and structure of the earth are termed), to come to important conclusions on many points connected with the subject of this investigation. And if we include, as the subject of our book allows, the inhabitants of shells, how wide a field of usefulness opens before us. How many thousands of our industrious population depend wholly, or in part, upon the capture and sale of shell-fish for their support. In some parts, as the western and northern Islands of Scotland, they have in times of scarcity afforded sustenance to the dwellers on the bleak and barren shores, who but for them must have perished. But of all this we shall have more to say when we come to describe the different members of the testaceous family. We will now offer a few remarks upon

## THE INHABITANTS OF SHELLS;

Which belong to that division of Natural History called the *Mollusca*, from the Latin *Mollis*— soft; these *Molluscous* animals, then, are animals having a soft body, and no internal skeleton. You may be quite sure that a *Mollusk* will never break its bones, because it has none to break; it has a shell, however, which may be broken, at least in some cases, for all *Mollusks* have not snug habitations of the kind; but wander about the watery or earthy world in which they live, quite naked; such as the sea and land slugs, and some worms, leeches, etc.; but with these we have nothing to do, our present subject including only a part of

## MALACOLOGY,

another member of that queer ology family, deriving its name from two Greek words signifying soft, and a discourse; hence it means a discourse upon soft, or soft-bodied animals, that is *mollusca.* It is only a part, then, of *Malacology* that we have to do with; that part which relates to the shell-inhabiting mollusks, and strange creatures enough some of these are. We will have a look at them presently; just now it will be sufficient to observe that the *mollusca testacea,* or soft-bodied animals, furnished with shells, possess the power of exuding, that is, discharging from various parts of their bodies a sticky kind of fluid, which mixing with the chalky matter collected from the water, and becoming hard, forms, in process of time, the shelly covering which is at once a dwelling and a defence for the inhabitant.

Miss Pratt, in her delightful book on " Common Things of the Sea Coast," observes of these shells that, " We gather up those which we find, and looking at their structure would fain know something of the inmate of such a dwelling. All nature proclaims the goodness of God. We hear that the bird which wings its way over our heads has a song of joy; the bee hums delightedly by us; and the little shrimp which darts in the clear pool, seems full of merriment. Was the inmate of the shell less cared for by its Maker? No doubt the little builder had some sense of joy, as he framed from his own substance the house which excites our admiration. Doubtless his existence, short and sluggish as it was, had its own consciousness of pleasure; and obscure as is his history, and little calculated as such a creature might seem to perform an important part in the economy of creation, yet we know that he had a work to do, not only for the living creatures of the sea, but for the well-being of man himself."

## CLASSIFICATION OF SHELLS.

The great naturalist, Linnæus, divided shells into thirty-six genera, each of which comprised a number of species; of these species somewhere about two thousand five hundred have been described and classified; the varieties, more or less distinct, are almost countless. Of shells found on and about the British Isles, there are about five hundred and fifty species, or, we should rather say were, for diligent inquirers into this branch of Natural History are almost daily adding to the number.

We have already seen that shells are sometimes called *Crystalline,* and sometimes *Granular,* in accordance with certain peculiarities of construction before mentioned: this is one mode of division. There are several others made use of in different systems of arrangement, which only a deeper study of the subject than can be here entered upon would enable one to understand; the plainest and most common, however, is that which has reference to the form of the shell, which is one of these—

| UNIVALVE. | BIVALVE. | MULTIVALVE. |
|---|---|---|

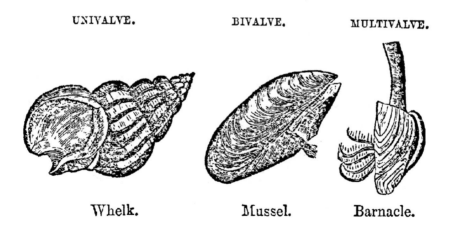

| Whelk. | Mussel. | Barnacle. |
|---|---|---|

These words are derived from the Latin, *unus*—one, *bi*—two, *multus*—many, and therefore it may at once be seen that they apply to shells having one, two, or several pieces or divisions. Valve comes from the Latin *valva*, and means a folding door, a lid, a piece moving on a hinge, as the divisions in several of these shells do.

This order of arrangement is generally followed by those who make a collection of shells for a cabinet; and to this we shall adhere, as at once the most simple and convenient, when we come to describe the several species of testaceous mollusks. We will now say a few words on

## TAKING AND PRESERVING SHELLS.

A diligent searcher along any beach or coast line will be sure sometimes to light upon curious and valuable specimens, and especially after violent storms may such be sought for, with the greatest chance of success, for the agitation of the waters will then have loosened them from their natural beds and dwelling-places, and cast them on the shore. Very frequently, however, they will be so beaten about and defaced, that they will be comparatively valueless; if enveloped in tangled masses of sea-weed, they are likely to be preserved from injury; and such heaps of uprooted marine vegetation will often afford a rich harvest to the young conchologist, who should always carefully examine them. Many of the shells are so minute as scarcely to be seen with the naked eye, therefore this search can scarcely be properly effected without the assistance of a pocket lens, the cost of which is but trifling. The undersides of pieces of stranded timber, the bottoms of boats lately returned from a fishing voyage, the fisherman's dredge or net, the cable, and the deep-sea line; all these may prove productive, and should be looked to whenever opportunity offers; nor should the search for land and fresh-water shells be neglected, for many of these are very curious, as well as beautiful, and no conchological collection is complete without them. For these, the best hunting-grounds are the ditch side and the river bed, the mossy bank and the hedge-row; amid the twining, serpent-like roots of the old thorn and elder trees; the crevices of the garden wall, the undersides of stones, and all sorts of out-of-the-way holes, nooks, and corners, where may be found the Striped Zebra, and other prettily-marked snail shells, and many other kinds worthy of a place in—

## THE CABINET,

which may be either large or small, plain or handsome, in accordance with the means of the collector. Perhaps for a beginner just a nest of shallow
drawers in a deal or other case may be quite
sufficient; these drawers should be divided into
compartments, on the front side of each of which
should be pasted a neatly-written label, with the
common and scientific name of the species of shell
contained in it, together with brief mention of the
date when, and the place where, it was taken ; and
any observations relating to it which can be comprised in a few words, and may seem to the
collector of sufficient interest to warrant their
insertion. This would be a good beginning; by
and by, when the collection is large, the knowledge
more ample, and the outlay can be spared, it will
be time to think of something ornamental—
mahogany and glass, and carved or inlaid work, such
a Cabinet as would properly display and enhance
the beauties of your testaceous treasures, which
are too often stowed away, with other natural
curiosities, in a very disorderly, higgledy-piggledy
sort of manner, like the collection described by
Dryden—

"He furnishes his closet first, and fills
    The crowded shelves with rarities of shells;
    Adds orient pearls, which from the wave he drew,
    And all the sparkling stones of various hue."

When live shells, as they are called—that is, having the living fish in them—are obtained, the best plan is to place them in spirits of wine; this at once deprives the inhabitant of life, without injuring the shell, which should then be placed in hot water for a time; the body of the mollusk is thus rendered firm, and may be removed by means of some pointed instrument. Care should be taken to leave no portion of animal matter within, or after a while it will become putrid, and give out a stain, which will show through and injure the delicate markings of the shell. The surest, most expeditious, and least troublesome mode of cleansing a shell, is to place it in an ant heap for a day or two; the busy little insects will penetrate into its inmost cavities, and remove hence all offending matter. There will be no difficulty in this respect with the multivalve and bivalve kinds, which are only kept closed by means of a set of muscles, which can be tightened or relaxed at the pleasure of the animal within, and become powerless to keep the shell closed as soon as that is dead.

Great care must be taken to preserve unbroken the smaller parts of these shells, such as the hinges or teeth, as on the structure of these the scientific arrangement into genera chiefly depends; the beard, also, as it is called, and silky threads, must not be removed, as these have much to do in determining the particular species.

River and land shells are generally very thin and brittle, and must be carefully handled; their colours are not usually so brilliant as those of the marine species, but they form links in the testaceous chain, which are necessary to a proper study and elucidation of conchology.

The most glowing and gorgeous of all shells are those brought from the Tropical seas, and, excepting in a few rare instances, specimens of most of these can be obtained at little cost from any dealer, or from sailors returning from a voyage. If it is necessary to send either those, or British shells, any distance, or to pack them away in a small compass, the best plan is to wrap them separately in soft paper, place them in a box, and then pour in sawdust, bran, or fine sand, very dry, until all the open spaces are completely filled up.

## ON CLEANING AND POLISHING SHELLS.

All shells, whether inhabited or not, when taken, should be soaked for a while in hot water, to remove the dirt which may adhere to them, and dissolve the saline (that is, salt) particles contained in the sea water; they should then be thoroughly dried, and if, as is the case with many, they naturally possess a good polish, they are at once fit for the cabinet. Generally, however, it happens that when shells are dry, they lose much of the peculiar brilliancy of hue which they possess when seen through the medium of the glistening water; to restore this, wash them over with a thin solution of gum arabic, or white of egg. Some collectors use a varnish made of gum mastic, dissolved in spirits of wine; this is, perhaps, preferable, as it is not affected by moisture. Many shells have a very plain, dull appearance, in consequence of being covered over with a kind of skin called an epidermis, a word derived from the Greek, and signifying the outer skin, sometimes called the cuticle. To remove this, soak the shell in warm water for some time, and then rub it over with a stiff brush until the covering is removed; should this be very thick, it will be necessary to mix a little nitric acid with the water; but this must be done very cautiously, for if too strong it will remove all the lustre from the surface of the shell subjected to its influence. Sometimes the file, and a substance called pumice-stone, has to be used, but these are dangerous agents in inexperienced hands. The best polish for the shell, after the skin is removed, is a red earth called tripoli, applied on a piece of soft leather.

## FOSSIL SHELLS.

An eminent geologist, named Dr. Mantell, has very beautifully and poetically termed rocks "the Medals of Creation." As on coins and medals we see stamped enduring records of great historical events, so upon the rocks are written by the finger of God a history of some of the mighty changes which the earth has undergone, and fossil shells are among the plainest and most easily read of the characters or letters in which these truths are written. As Dr. Harvey, in his "Sea-side Book," observes, " Shelly-coated mollusca have existed in the waters of the sea, and in rivers, from a very early period of the world's history, and have left in its most stratified rocks and gravels abundance of their shells preserved in a more perfect manner than the remains of most other animals. Now, as the species in the early rocks differ from those found in later formations, quite as much as the latter from the mollusca of our modern seas, the gradual change in the character of the embedded shells marks a certain interval of time in the world's history." So we see that these rocks are the leaves of a great book, written all over with wonderful truths, and those who study such sciences as Geology and Conchology, are enabled to read much that is there written.

Every fossil shell that such a student picks out of the chalk, or limestone, is like a letter in the Alphabet of Creation; it has a significance, or meaning, and a number of such put together form, as it were, words and sentences, that can be made up into chapters, full of instruction, aye, and of amusement too. The study may seem a little dry at first, but never mind, go on, and you will soon be rewarded for your diligence by the wonders that will unfold themselves to your understanding —the fresh and delightful views which you will obtain into the wide universe, the new and enlarged ideas of the wisdom and goodness of the Creator, and of the formation, habits, and connection each with each of his various creatures.

Properly to treat of fossil shells would require a book of itself, and a large book too; we can here but allude to the subject, as a part, and a very important and interesting part, of the study of Conchology; more will be said about it in a volume which we purpose writing for this series, on Rocks, and the petrified organic remains found in and about them.

" Those relics of an older world, which tell
    Of changes slow or sudden, that have past
Over the face of Nature; fossil shell,
    Shark's tooth, and bone of megatheran vast,
Turned into stone, and so preserved to show
Man of those things whereof he ought to know."

# UNIVALVES.

GASTEROPODA is a name given by some naturalists to a very extensive group of molluscous animals; the term is derived from two Greek words, signifying stomach and foot;—it has reference to the kind of fleshy foot which generally occupies the whole under side of the body, and by the contraction and extension of the muscles of which, the creature is enabled to glide, with a slow but steady motion, from place to place. The Slug and the Snail are the commonest examples which can be adduced of *gasteropods*; and one may tell by their slimy tracks, shining like silver in the morning sunshine, that during the night, which is their principal feeding-time, they manage to get over a considerable extent of ground, although "a snail's gallop" is a proverbial expression for slow motion; but it is astonishing how much work of any kind may be done if one "keeps at it"; by doing this the Tortoise beat the Hare, illustrating the truth of the proverb, that " slow and sure wins the race." If you watch a Snail travelling with its house upon its back, it does not seem to make much way, and you are inclined to think that it will be long ere it reaches the new settlement to which it appears journeying with bag and baggage; but leave the spot for a while, and the chances are that on your return, the "slow coach" will have got somewhere

out of sight. Here is a lesson for boys and girls; whatever you take in hand, don't be in a hurry, and if people say you are "slow," think of the Snail, and keep on!

This, then, is a shelled mollusk of the third class, called *Gasteropoda*, according to the system of the French naturalist Cuvier. It has a distinct head, which, like the hinder part of the body, which we may call a tail if we like, projects, when the creature is in motion, considerably from the shell; it is also furnished with what we commonly call horns, naturalists say *tentacles*, from the Latin *tento*—trying, or essaying; with these the creature, as it were, feels its way, being extremely sensitive; they answer the purpose of organs both of sight and touch; put your finger slowly towards one of them, and you will observe that, even before contact, it begins to retract, or draw in, as though sensible of the approach of some opposing body, as it no doubt is. These horns of the Snail, then, are its feelers—eyes to the blind, fingers to the finger-less; so God provides for his creatures all that may be necessary for their existence, and compensates for the deprivation of one sense or organ, by some admirable contrivance which meets the necessities of the case.*

* It appears likely that the little knobs at the end of the Snail's feelers, are, as some naturalists assert, in reality eyes; if so, we were wrong in calling the creature blind. Yet is their position and construction so different from organs of sight generally, that they serve rather to strengthen than invalidate the above observations. The number of the horns varies in different kinds of snails from two to six, and some have none at all. These tentacles, when present, are always situated above the mouth; some of them have the knobs at the base, others at the sides; and it has been conjectured that they may be organs of smell, as well as of sight and touch.

## THE COMMON SNAIL

Is called by naturalists *Helix aspersa*, the generic name being derived from a Greek work signifying spiral, and having reference to the shape of the shell; the plural is *Helices*, a term applied to all convoluted or twisted shells, which terminate in a point like a church spire: a spiral-shelled fossil is called a *helicate*. The specific name comes from the Latin *asper*—rough; whence also our English word *asperity*—roughness, and several others. The *Helicidæ*, or *Helix* family, is that which includes the land shell Snails and the naked Slugs, and in this family there are several genera; they are distinguished from the shelled water Snails, both sea and river, by having a different breathing apparatus, and some other points of internal construction which it is not necessary to describe here.

The Common Snail has a mouth, of which it makes good use, as market gardeners well know, and yet this mouth is not furnished with teeth; instead of these, the upper lip, which is of a horny texture, is what is called *dentated*, from the Latin *dentus*—a tooth, that is, divided or separated, so as to present somewhat the appearance of a row of teeth in the jaw; this lip is of an arched form, and appears to be a very serviceable kind of instrument to Mr. *Helix aspersa,* who, if his character be not *aspersed,* is very des'ructive to all sorts of greenery. The lower lip is divided only in the middle, where there is an opening of some width: it is not horny, like the upper one.

Snails lay eggs, which are about the size of very small peas; they are soft, and of a whitish colour. Being semi, that is, half, transparent, or clear, their contents can be partly seen; and in those of a water Snail, deposited against the side of a glass bottle, the young were detected with partially-formed shells upon their backs.

To show how tenacious they are of life, it has been mentioned that Mr. S. Simon, a Dublin merchant, had a collection of fossils and other curiosities left him by his father; among these were some shells of Snails, and *fifteen years* after the collection came into his possession, his son had the shells to play with, and placed them in a basin of water, when lo! out came the slimy bodies and knobbed horns of several of the *Gasteropods,* no doubt hungry enough after their long sleep.

We all know that our Common Snails hybernate, or sleep through the winter. As soon as the chills of autumn are felt, they seek out some snug crevice

in an old wall, or burrow in the earth, or congre-
gate beneath garden pots, roots of trees, thatched
roofs, or in any hole or corner that may be convenient, and then throwing a kind of temporary
skin, like a drum head, which naturalists call *operculum,* over the opening of their shells, and sticking
themselves fast to the sides of their refuge, or to
each other, they sleep away, careless of frosts and
tempests.

A moist and rather warm state of the atmosphere
seems most congenial to the land Snails, some
species of which are found in all countries, except
those where the most intense cold prevails. Generally speaking, they do not like dry heat, and to
escape from it will get under stones, and into other
cool places, from whence a shower brings them
forth in such numbers, the smaller species especially, as to lead to the popular belief that it sometimes rains Snails.

These *Gasteropods,* although extremely injurious
to vegetation, must not be regarded as worse than
useless, as they commonly are; besides furnishing
food for several wild, as well as domesticated, birds,
they are no doubt a nourishing article of diet for
man. The Romans had their *cochlearia,* where
Snails were regularly fed and fattened for the table;

and the French at the present day their *escargo-toires,* or Snailery, for the same purpose; some of the Snails so kept attain an immense size, as well they may if fed, as by the Romans, on new wine and meal. Many poor persons, especially those who are consumptive, might no doubt derive much cheap sustenance and benefit from using the larger species of *Helicidæ,* which might be collected from hedges and gardens as food. Why should they not eat those as well as the marine mollusks, such as Oysters, Cockles, Whelks, etc.?

Snails have an extraordinary power of re-pro-ducing any part which may be injured or cut off, even to the extent of the whole head, as has been observed to be the case; the reparation of injury done to the shell they can effect easily, as can all testaceous mollusks. Respecting the construction of the shell, it may be observed that it is produced in the thickness of the mantle, or cloak-like covering, which envelops the body of the animal; the forma-tion commences at the small end or spire, and gradually goes on, whorl upon whorl, as the still widening circles which gives the ridgy appearance to most univalves are called. *Columella,* or *pillar,* is the name given to the spire on which the cones are rolled; this is sometimes solid and sometimes hollow; when the latter, the open end is called the *Umbilicus,* meaning the navel or centre. The opening at the bottom, from which the animal issues, is the last portion finished, and this is called the *aperture,* a Latin word adopted into the English dictionary. Some of these *Helices* are wide and flat, even hollow and cup-like, with the whorls rising above the pillar—these are called *discoid* shells;

DISCOID.                    TURBINATED.

others which are long and narrow, with projecting spires, are termed *turbinated* shells: the former being more or less flat or disk-like, the latter twisted, whirling, like a spinning-top, from the Latin *turbo*—a whirling, a turning round.

If we take a Common Snail, and plunge it into boiling water, which will instantly kill it, so that it can be removed from the shell, we shall find the whole of that part of the body which was lodged in the upper whorls, or spiral part of the shell, is covered with a thin membrane or skin; this is called the *mantle,* and that portion of it which corresponds with what we may consider as the back of the mollusk, and which is considerably thickened, is termed the *collar;* here are situated the glands, which secrete the colouring and other matter of which the shell is mainly composed; although the substance called nacre, or mother-of-pearl, is secreted in the thinner part of the mantle; it is however from the collar that the growth or increase of the shell proceeds. It is in accordance with certain variations in the shape and disposition of this mantle and collar, that shells assume such very different shapes. Sometimes the whorls or spiral ridges, are projected or thrown far out, and this produces the *turbinated* shell. Sometimes they scarcely rise above each other, but rather spread towards the sides, and then we have the *discoid* shape. Generally speaking, the whorls of a shell take a direction from left to right, but occasionally an opposite one; they are then called sinistral, or left-handed shells; such are not common. If one of the twisted shells be divided lengthways, it will be seen that the inside of the whorls wind in an ascending direction, round the *Columella* or central column, as the spiral staircases in the Crystal Palace.

But let us return to our Garden Snail, who has many near relatives in Britain, several of which have beautifully-marked and convoluted shells, as will be seen by a reference to our coloured illustrations, Plate I. We will introduce them in due order. Fig. 1, the Banded Snail (*Helix nemoralis*), from the Latin *nemus*—a wood or grove; the prettily-striped shells of this species may be found in great plenty among the roots and in the crevices of the rugged boles of old forest trees, as well as in hedge-rows and in mossy banks, and other situations near woods. Fig. 2, the Heath Snail (*H. ericetorum*), from *erica*, the Latin for heath; a small species with brown bands, remarkable for its large *umbilicus*, perforating the centre of the shell nearly through. Fig. 3, the Silky Snail (*H. sericea*), from the Latin *sericus*—silk-like; the shell of this species is covered with short slimy hairs, which give it a glistening appearance. Fig. 4, the Stone Snail (*H. lapicida*), from the Latin *lapis*—a stone: Linnæus called the species the Stone Cutter, probably on account of its habit of frequenting stony places, and the peculiar construction of the shell, which has a sharp edge running round each whorl; it is commonly found lodged in the cavities of loose-lying stones, but which it can scarcely be suspected of having hollowed out for its own accommodation. Fig. 5, the Elegant Cyclostome (*Cyclostoma elegans*). On turning to the dictionary, we find that *cyclostomous* means having a circular mouth. This species is sometimes called *Turbo elegans*; the beautifully-marked shells are often found in chalky hills covered with brushwood. This pretty mollusk has a curious mode of travelling; the under surface of the foot, which is long, is divided by a deep fissure into two narrow strips, like ribbons; these take hold of whatever the creature may be moving on alternately; one keeping fast hold while the other advances, in like manner to fix itself, and drag the body forward. Fig. 6, the Undulated Plekochcilos (*P. undulatus*); the Latin *plecto*—to twist or twine, seems to be the root from which the generic name of this Snail is derived; the specific name will be easily understood; to undulate, is to flow like waves, and the lines on the shell it will be seen are undulating. This is not a British species, but is introduced here to give variety to the group; it is a West Indian Mollusk, and is found in immense numbers in the forests of St. Vincent; it glues its eggs to the leaves of a plant which holds water, and thus secures for them a damp atmosphere at all times. And here we must conclude our chapter of Land Snails, leaving unnoticed very many beautiful and interesting species, both British and Foreign.

Many poets have alluded to the Snail, but we can only find room for a few verses by Cowper :—

To grass, or leaf, or fruit, or wall,
The snail sticks close, nor fears to fall,
As if he grew there, house and all
            Together.

Within that house secure he hides,
When danger imminent betides
Of storm, or other harm besides,
            Of weather.

Give but his horns the slightest touch,
His self-collecting power is such,
He shrinks into his house with much
            Displeasure.

Where'er he dwells, he dwells alone,
Except himself has chattels none,
Well satisfied to be his own
            Whole treasure.

Thus hermit-like, his life he leads,
Nor partner of his banquet needs,
And if he meets one only feeds
            The faster.

Who seeks him must be worse than blind
(He and his house are so combin'd),
If, finding it, he fails to find
　　　　　　　Its master.

———

## FRESH-WATER SHELLS.

Many of the following group of Fresh-water
Shells, are remarkable for elegance of form, and
some for richness of colouring; hence, perhaps, the
scientific name applied to the family in which they
are mostly included—*Limnœidœ*, which, like *limn*—
to paint, agrees with the French *enluminer*.  These

mollusks are found in rivers, streams, ditches, and
moist marshy places.  Like those which live wholly
on land, they breathe through lungs, and therefore
cannot exist without air; which accounts for their
frequently coming to the surface, when under

water. In brooks, as well as in stagnant pools, which abound with aquatic plants, they may be found in vast numbers, feeding upon the moist vegetation.

The Common Limnea (*L. stagnalis*) is mostly an inhabitant of stagnant waters, where it is often seen floating with the shell reversed, as in a boat; this shell, like most of those of the Fresh-water Mollusks, is thin, and easily broken; the shape, it

will be seen, is peculiarly elegant, the spire being slender and pointed—very different from that of the Spreading Limnea, called by naturalists, *L. auricularia*, from *aurus*—the ear, to which the broad aperture, or opening of the shell, may be compared; this resembles the other species in its habits. The Horny Planorbis, in Latin *P. corneus*, from *cornu*—a horn. The shape, you will see, is flat, the whorls rolling upon each other like the

3

Patel

folds of a bugle horn; this shape would be termed orbicular, from *orbis*—a sphere, or circular body. This is the largest European species of Fresh-water Shells so constructed; it is often found in deep clear ditches, and yields a beautiful purple dye, which, however, soon becomes dull, and changes; it cannot be fixed, and is therefore valueless. The mouth of this shell, in fine specimens, is tinged with pale violet or lilac.

There is another kind, the Keeled Planorbis (*P. lurinatus*), which has the outer edge of the shell

finely ridged, or keeled; it is very small, and very plentiful in fresh-water, both running and stagnant; where, too, is found the Common Physa (*P. fontinalis*), the latter word meaning a spring or fountain. This little mollusk is a quick and active traveller, it sometimes comes out of its shell and throws itself about in an extraordinary way, keeping fast hold by its foot; the generic name, *Physa,* would seem to have reference to the round,

smooth, delicate shell, and to come from the same
root as *Physalite,* which means a topaz : the members
of this genus are very numerous, being found nearly
all over the globe.   The next belongs to the family
*Auriculadæ,* or Ear Shells.   The Midas' Ear (*A.
Midæ*), this handsome shell is prized by collectors ;
it comes from the East Indies.   Midas, it is said,
was one who set himself up for a judge of music in
the old fabulous times, and not appreciating that of
Apollo, was rewarded by the angry god with a pair
of ass's ears.

The Cone-shaped Melampus (*M. corniformis*),
also an Ear Shell, is found in the rivers of the
Antilles Islands.   It is a pretty shell; the formation
is much the same as that of many of the most highly-
prized varieties of Marine Shells ; of these we shall
have to speak presently.   *Melampodium* in Latin,
signifies a poisonous plant called Black Hellebore ;
in the Mythology, *Melampus* was a great magician,
who did all sorts of wonderful things;  but we
cannot tell what relation there exists between either
the plant or the magician and this pretty cone shell.
To give variety to this group, we will now throw in
a land species called *Megaspira Ruschenbergiana,*
about the origin of whose name we cannot even
hazard a guess; the termination of the generic name,

you will see is *spira,* and a glance at the shell will at once suggest a reason for this; its long tapering spire consists of twenty-three closely-set gradually increasing whorls. This is a rare shell, whose

inhabitant has not yet been described by naturalists; several of the marine species closely resemble it in shape. Much more might be said about the Land and Fresh-water Shells, but we must here leave them, having a wide field before us—namely, the Sea or Marine *Testacea,* one of the most common of which is

## THE WHELK,

A univalve shell inhabited by a gasteropod mollusk, or, we should rather say, naturally so tenanted, for very frequently it is taken possession of by the Soldier or Hermit Crab, which having no hard covering to protect their soft plump bodies, are obliged to take lodgings where they can get them, and generally prefer the Whelk shell, of which we here give a figure.

This is one of the commonest of our Marine

Mollusks; it is called by naturalists *Buccinum un-
datum;* the first, or generic term, being the Latin
for a trumpet, and the second, or specific name,
meaning waved, or, as we often say, undulated.
So we call this the Waved Whelk; fishermen term

it the Conch, or the Buckie, and tell strange stories
of its ravenous appetite and murderous propensities;
how, with its spiny tongue, situated at the end of
a long flexible proboscis or trunk, it drills a hole in
the shell of the Oyster, or other testacean, and
sucks out the contents; empty shells, so drilled,
are frequently found on the shore, and often, when
the dredge is let down into an oyster bed, it comes
up time after time filled with Whelks, of which
such numbers are sometimes taken, that they are
sold to the farmers to be used as manure for the
soil. This mollusk is a favourite article of food
with the poorer classes of our land, but it is hard
and indigestible. The shell may frequently be
found in large numbers among the beach stones;

it is strong and firm, from three to four inches long, of a dirty yellowish white. There are two other Whelks common upon our coasts—the Stone or Dog Whelk (*B. lapillus*), from the Latin *lapis*—a stone; and *B. reticulatum*, so called because the shell is *reticulated*, or marked with many lines crossing each other, like net-work; it comes from the Latin *reticulum*—a net; hence also we have *reticule*—a small work-bag, at one time very much carried by ladies.

———

## ROCK SHELLS,

Are so called on account of their rough and wrinkled forms; they are nearly allied to the Whelks, to which they bear a close resemblance. Several species are found on our shores, the most common being the Humble Murex (*M. despectus*), from the Latin *despecto*—to despise; this is often used by the fishermen for bait. Some of the foreign Rock Shells are very curious and beautiful; three of them will be found on Plate II., Figs. 1, 2, and 3. The Common Thorny Woodcock (*M. tribulus*), from the French for trouble, whence we have also tribulation, which is sometimes said to be a thorny path. This curious shell is also called Venus' Comb. It is found in the Indian Ocean, from whence it is also brought. Fig. 2, the Woodcock's Head (*M. haustellum*), from the Latin *haustus*—a draught; the bill of the Woodcock being adapted for sucking. This term is also applied to insects that live by suction. The shell, it will be seen, is destitute of spines, but it is ribbed and beautifully marked. Fig. 3 is worthy of its name—the Royal Murex (*M. regius*), from *regno*—to reign. It is a splendid species, of the rich colouring of which art can give but a faint impression. It is brought from the western coast of Central and South America, where, as well as in the islands of the South Pacific, many new shells of the genus *Murex* have been discovered.

One shell found on our own coast, often mistaken for a Whelk, is the Pelican's-foot Strombus, called in scientific language, *Strombus pes-pelicanus*, which is but a Latinized form of the English name. This shell varies greatly in shape in different stages of its growth, and by an inexperienced conchologist, the young, middle-aged, and old Strombus might be taken for distinct species. In the *Strombidæ* family, so called we know not why, the same word in Latin meaning a kind of shell-fish, are some species which have produced pearls. One member of the family which we sometimes see in collections, is a large and very beautiful shell; this is the Broad-winged Strombus (*S. latissimus*), probably from *latesco*—to wax or grow broad, or large; *issimus* being in the superlative degree, would indicate that

this shell was very much so, as we find it is, some-times measuring as much as twelve inches across. In Plate II. is a representation of this handsome shell, greatly reduced in size, of course. See Fig. 4. We here give a figure, as more curious than beauti-ful, of the Scorpion Pteroceras (*P. scorpius*), which

CHINESE SPINDLE.

also belongs to the *Strombidæ* family; as does the curious Chinese Spindle (*Rostellaria rectirostris*). The generic name of the first of these species comes from the Greek *Ptero*, pronounced *tero*, meaning a wing, and *cerus*—waxen. Both the generic and specific names of the second refer to the peculiar conformation of the shell, being derived from the Latin, and meaning a straight line or beak.

On Plate III. will be found the Imbricated Purpura (*P. imbricata*), Fig. 1, which claims a close alliance with the Whelks. The generic name has reference to the dye yielded by this, as well as all the shells of the genus; the specific name comes from the Latin *imbrex*—the gutter-tile ; thus *imbricated*, a term often used in Natural History, means ridged, like the roof of a house, where the tiles are placed to overlap each other, so that the rain will run off. The Persian Purpura, or, as it is called in Latin, *Purpura Persica*, Fig. 2, is another handsome shell of this family group ; its name indicates the place where it is found. The other species described comes from South America, and the *P. lapillus* (the meaning of the specific name has already been explained), is common on our shores, being found in great abundance on the rocks at low water. We read in Scripture of Tyrian purple, and there is every reason to suppose that the rich colour was obtained from these and other shell-fish.

## PERIWINKLE.

This is the commonest representative which we have of the family *Turbinidæ*, which comprehends, according to Cuvier, all the species which have the shell completely and regularly *turbinated*—that is, if we translate the Latin word into English, twisted. The little Periwinkle (here he is) is by no means a handsome mollusk, but some of his relatives are very beautiful, as we shall presently show. He is called by naturalists *T. littoreus*—from *littoralis*, belonging to the shore —and is often eaten by boys and girls with great relish; but he is not very digestible, and sometimes occasions dangerous disorders. The Swedish peasants believe that when the periwinkle crawls high upon the rocks, a storm is brewing from the south; but Linnæus quotes a Norwegian author to show that according to popular belief, it foretells the approach of a land wind with a calm on shore. Man may learn much of elemental changes from an observation of the movements and habits of all living creatures, which are instructed by God to provide for their safety and wants, and often perceive, long before man himself does, the indications of calm and tempest, rain and drought, etc. But our little *Turbo*, what of him? will you boil him, and pick out his curled-up form with a pin? or let him go crawling about the rocks, feeding upon the delicate earlier growth of marine vegetation? In the former case, you will have to reject the little kind of horny scale attached to his foot, which forms, when he retires into his habitation, a closely-fitting door to make all snug.

Several species of this genus are found on our shores; one of those is the *Turbo rudis*, or Red Turbo, which has a very thick periwinkle-like shell, about three-quarters of an inch long; the colour is dull red, fawn, or drab.

Of the foreign *Turbinæ*, sometimes called Turban Shells, we will now introduce two or three species, which will be found on Plate III. Fig. 3 is the Marbled Turbo (*T. marmoratus*), from the Latin *marmor*—marble; a large handsome shell well known to conchologists, and a native of the Indian seas. Fig. 4 is the Twisted Turbo (*T. torquatus*); this shell, when deprived of its outer coat or layer, is beautifully *nacreous*, or, if we may so speak, mother-of-pearly. The specimens which have reached England were brought from King

George's Sound. Fig. 5 is called Cook's Turbo (*T. Cookii*); this is a handsome South Sea shell, oftentimes of large size. It has been found in great numbers on the coast of New Zealand.

On Plate IV. we have placed two very curiously formed and marked shells, called Wentletraps, also belonging to the family *Turbinidæ*. The scientific name is *Scalaria*, from the Latin *scala*—a ladder, which the ribbed shells are supposed to resemble. Of this genus there are about eighty distinct species known; they are mostly deep-sea shells found in warm latitudes, although several inhabit the European seas, and one, the Common False Wentletrap (*S. communis*), Fig. 1, may often be picked up on our own shores. Fig. 2, the Royal Staircase Wentletrap, is a rare and valuable shell, generally brought from India and China; the scientific name is *S. pretiosa*, given to it by the French naturalist Lamarck, on account of the high price which it fetched; *pretiose*, in Latin, meaning costly, valuable. As much as £100 have been given for a single specimen of this shell; and a fine one, especially if it exceed two inches in length, yet commands a considerable sum, although not nearly so much as that. A good deal like the False Wentletrap in general outline, is the Awl-shaped Turritella, found in the African and Indian Seas. This is the *T. terebra* of naturalists; the first name referring to the turret shape common to the genus, and the last being the Latin word for an auger, or piercer. The Roseate Turritella (*T. rosea*) is also sometimes seen in collections; the beautiful rosy tint of the live shell changes to a dull red or brown, on the death of the mollusk.

———

## TROCHUS, OR TOP-SHELL.

" Of the shelled Mollusca which the dredge ever and anon brings up," says Mr. Gosse, in his delightful volume on the *Aquarium*, or *Aquavivarium*, as the glass tank in which living marine animals and vegetables are kept, is called, from the Latin *aqua*—water, and *vivo*—to live, " the *Trochi* are among the most conspicuous for beauty. The chief glory of this genus is the richly-painted internal surface of their shells, in which they are not excelled by any even of the true margaritiferous or pearly bivalves."

Of this *Trochidæ* family, a few of the members must be introduced to our readers; it is rather a numerous one, consisting of more than one hundred species, which are scattered nearly all over the world, few seas being without some of them. They are found at various depths, from near the surface to forty-five fathoms down, creeping on rocks, sand, masses of sea-weed, etc. We will first speak of those found on our own shores, the two commonest, as well as the smallest of which, are the Grey and the Spotted Trochi, scientifically named *T. cincrarius* and *T. maculata,* the translation of the first Latin specific name being ashy or ash-coloured, and that of the second, spotted. *Trochus,* in the same language, signifies a top, and has reference to the shape of most of these shells, which are something like a boy's whip-top.

Children on the coast sometimes call the last-named of the above species Pepper-and-salt Shells, because in colour they resemble the cloth so named. The Muddy-red Trochus (*T. ziziphinus*), so called, perhaps, because in colour it resembles the ziziphia, or fruit of the jujube tree, is also common with us. This shell is about an inch long, of a grey tint dashed with dark spots, these follow the line of the spiral turnings, which are very regular, proceeding from the opening below to the apex or point. Seen on shore, its colours are dull and faint, but beneath the water, inhabited by a living mollusk, it looks as though made of pearl, and studded with rubies; the animal, too, is richly coloured, being yellow with black stripes. See Plate IV., Fig. 3.

Not so common as the last is another British mollusk of this genus, called the Granulated Trochus (*T. granulatus*). It is the larger, and, as many think, the more elegant shell of the two, being in colour a faint flesh tint or yellowish white, shaded here and there with purple; the spiral lines which encircle it are composed of small round knobs which stand out like beads.

There is a singular shell of this genus, called the Carrier Trochus (*T. phorus*); it is generally found loaded with foreign objects, such as shells, small stones, bits of coral, etc., which it attaches to itself, and so goes about like a collector of natural curiosities, with his cabinet on his back.

The Imperial Trochus (*T. imperialis*), Fig. 4, whose scientific name explains itself, is one of the handsomest shells of the genus; it is very rare, and has hitherto been found only at New Zealand. Let us give our young readers a specimen of the way in which scientific writers describe shells; thus, this foreign Trochus, they tell us, is "orbicularly conical, the apex obtuse, the whorls turgidly

convex, squamose, radiate at the margin." This
is quite a simple affair to some descriptions, and
simple in fact it is to one, who, by attentive study,
has become familiarized with the meaning of the
terms. To one also who is acquainted with the
Greek and Latin tongues, they will be sufficiently
plain, although he has never seen them applied
before, for they are all derived from those dead
languages, as they are called, and so convey their
own meaning to every educated naturalist, no
matter of what nation he may be; and hence their
chief value. It is not necessary for our readers to
trouble themselves about the meaning of such terms
at present; by and by it will be necessary for them
to do so, if they wish to prosecute the study of
any natural science.

But about the Imperial Trochus, with its "orbicularly conical" shell—that term we may explain
as round and cone-like; a reference to Fig. 4,
Plate IV., will show what is meant by this more
clearly than words can, and likewise exhibit the
beautiful markings of this species, with its ground
tint of rich violet-brown. This beauty is often
obscured by calcareous incrustations and marine
plants, showing that the mollusk is sluggish in its
habits—a slothful creature. So it is with human

beings, sloth covers and hides the good qualities and virtues with an overgrowth at all times difficult to remove, and oftentimes destructive of all that is fair and good in the character.—Children, be not slothful! The Obelisk Trochus (*T. obeliscus*), is a rare white and green shell, sometimes seen in collections; it is of a conico-pyramidal form, not remarkable for beauty, and is a native of the Indian seas.

Mr. Gosse speaks of the Tops and Winkles as among the most useful inhabitants of the Aquarium; they mow down with their rasping tongues the thick growth of *Confervæ*, which would otherwise spread like a green curtain over the glass walls of the tank, and obstruct the view of its inhabitants. Here is this author's description of the beautiful piece of mechanism by which this work is effected :— "The appearance and position of the organ would surprise any one who searched for it for the first time ; and as it is easily found, and as Periwinkles are no rarities, let me commend it to your examination. The easiest mode of extracting it, supposing you are looking for *it* alone, is to slit the thick muzzle between the two tentacles, when the point of a needle will catch and draw out what looks like a slender white thread, two inches or more in length, one end of which is attached to the throat, and the

other, which is free, you will see coiled in a beautiful spiral manner, within the cavity of the stomach.

By allowing this tiny thread to stretch itself on a plate of glass, which is easily done by putting a drop of water on it first, which may then be drained off and dried, you will find that it is in reality an excessively delicate ribbon of transparent cartilaginous substance or membrane, on which are set spinous teeth of glassy texture and brilliancy. They are perfectly regular, and arranged in three rows, of which the middle ones are three-pointed, while on each of the outer rows a three-pointed tooth alternates with a larger curved one, somewhat boat-like in form. All the teeth project from the surface of the tongue on hooked curves, and all point in the same direction."

And with this curious piece of mechanism the little Winkle works away and cuts down swathe after swathe of the minute vegetation, just as a mower does the meadow grass; only the mollusk eats as he goes, and so gets payment for his labour; the man has it in another and to him more useful form. We might tell a very long story about these Tops and Winkles, which are nearly related to each other, but must now pass on to describe the rest of

5

the shells on Plate IV., which are the Perspective Solarium (*S. perspectivum*), Fig. 5, the generic name comes from *sol*—the sun, and viewed perspectively, that is, in such a position that the whole top of the shell is at once presented to the view, looking like a flat surface, it presents a circular appearance, marked with rings and rays like representations of the sun sometimes do.

The Variegated Solarium (*S. variegatum*), Fig. 6, is a small but very pretty shell, somewhat rare. The mollusk is remarkable on account of the singular shape of its operculum, which differs from that of all other species; it is of a cone-shape, and covered from top to bottom with what are called membranous lamellæ, that appear to stand out like little shelves winding up spirally. This singular form of operculum has been long known to naturalists, but it is not until lately that they have discovered to what species of testacean it belonged. Let us here explain that *operculus* is the Latin for a cover or lid.

## CONES, VOLUTES, MITRES, AND OLIVES.

These are names given by collectors to certain classes of univalve shells, distinguished by peculiarities of formation, more or less distinct. We shall describe two or three of each, that our readers may have some idea of the meaning of the terms which are often used by those who speak or write on conchology.

The family of Cones, called *Conidæ*, is an extensive one; considerably above two hundred species having been discovered. Many of them are very beautiful, both in shape and colour, so that they are highly valued by collectors; they are principally found in the southern and tropical seas, upon sandy bottoms, at depths varying from a few feet to seventeen fathoms. The shells are generally thick and solid, rolled up, as it were, into a conical form; the most familiar illustration that can be given of this form is a sugar-loaf, which all these shells more or less resemble in general outline, as thus—

Cones are either plain or coronated, that is, crowned, having rows of projections round the top of the shell, like the second of the above figures; and this forms a mark of division into two classes, although these classes often run, as it were, one into the other, some plain cones having slight irregularities of surface, and some crowned ones being very nearly plain.

The Common, or Ordinary Cone (*Conus generalis*), Plate V., Fig. 1, is an elegantly-shaped and beautifully-marked shell, having much the appearance of being carved out of some rare kind of marble. The Lettered Cone (*Conus littoralis*), Fig. 2, appears to be scribbled over with Hebrew, Greek, or Arabic characters, and almost every species has something peculiar in its markings; clouds and veins, and dots, and stripes, and bands, of every conceivable shape and mode of arrangement, may be met with in these shells, whose surface, when the epidermis or outer skin is removed, bears a beautiful polish. Curious names have been given to some of them, such, for instance, as the High Admiral, Vice Admiral, and Guinea Admiral, which indicate the rank they hold in the estimation of collectors. From five to twenty guineas is the price at which good and rare ones have been valued, and one, the *Conus cedo nulli,* which may be translated, the Cone second to none, has fetched the enormous sum of three hundred guineas. It must not bo supposed that these shells exhibit all their beauties when, inhabited by a carnivorous or flesh-eating mollusk, they move slowly about, or lie for a time motionless among the rocks and sand-beds of the ocean. The before-mentioned epidermis, which is the Latin for the outer skin of the human body, covers them like a cloak or mantle, which is the name it bears among naturalists. Much careful labour is required to bring them to a fit state for cabinet shells.

VOLUTES form an extensive family of shells under the name *Volutinæ.* The greater part are natives of tropical seas, and dwell far down, so that they are seldom found on the coast, except after storms. There are a few European species, but these are not remarkable for beauty, as most of the others are. The generic name signifies twisted, or rather wreathed, as flowers or leaves might be, about some central object. In these shells the spire is generally short, as it is in many cones, sometimes scarcely apparent; the form is usually elegant, and the markings often striking and handsome. On Plate V. will be found three examples—Fig. 3 is the Undulated Volute (*V. undulata*), the Latin for a little wave is *undula*, and these marks are like the lines caused by the flowing of the waves on a sandy shore: this shell is found chiefly in the South Pacific; the animal which inhabits it is prettily marked with zebra-like stripes. Fig. 4 is called the Pacific Volute (*V. Pacificus*), the shape, it will be seen, is somewhat different, being more angular, and it is without the waved lines. Fig. 5, the Bat Volute (*V. vespertilio*), is more decidedly knobbed or spiked, approaching nearly to the shape of some of the coronated ones. This species is found in the Indian seas; the specific name is the Latin for a bat.

MITRES. These are usually considered as a genus, or branch of the Volute family; the scientific name is *mitra*. The form is generally long, slender, and pointed, something like the bishop's mitre, hence the common name of the genus. In the Episcopal Mitre (*M. episcopalis*), Plate VI., Fig. 1, we see this form in its greatest perfection; this is a handsome shell, found in the Indian seas and on the coasts of the South Sea Islands. The mollusk is remarkable for a long proboscis, double the length of the shell, the extremity of which swells into a club form, and has an oval orifice or opening: the specific name, *episcopalis,* comes from the Latin, and means of, or like a bishop. The Tanned Mitre (*M. adusta*), from the Latin *adustus*—burned or parched, is what is called fusiform and turreted; that is, shaped like a spindle, and having a spire or turret-like termination. The streaks of colour are transverse, that is, running the length of the shell; or in other words, they are longitudinal. This, too, comes from the South Sea Islands. Fig. 2 is the Wrinkled Mitre (*M. corrugata*), from the Latin *corrugo*—to wrinkle. It is very different, both in shape and markings, from the last species; the whorls, it will be seen, are angulated or pointed above, and the lower part of the shell is much larger than the spiral or upper portion. It is a true mitre nevertheless, although not just such a one as a bishop would like to wear. It inhabits the Indian Ocean, the coast of New Guinea, etc.

OLIVES. These, for richness of colour and brilliancy of effect, will bear comparison with any genus of shells. Naturalists speak of them collectively as *Olivinæ.* They belong to the Volute family, and are said to number about eighty species. Most of those which have reached this country have come from the Mauritius, where they catch them with lines baited with portions of Cuttle-fish. We have here depicted two of them, namely, the Figured Olive, Fig. 3 (*Oliva textilina*), from the Latin *textilus*, which is woven or plaited; and the Ruddy Olive, Fig. 4 (*O. sanguinolenta*), from *sanguis*—blood.

We must now bring our notice of the Univalves to a conclusion. There are several genera and many very curious and beautiful species which we have been unable to notice at all, and of those which we have, a short account only could be given—sufficient, however, as we trust, to interest our readers in the subject, and induce them to continue the study of it into larger works. Before leaving this division of shells, we would call their attention to one of its greatest ornaments—that is, the Ventricose Harp Shell (*Harpa ventricosa*), from the Latin *ventriculus*—the stomach, applied to this shell on account of its swelled or inflated shape. Nothing, however, can be more elegant than the whole form, nor more beautiful than the markings of this lovely species (see Plate VI., Fig. 5), which belongs properly to the Whelk family.

## COWRIES.

Of Cowries we have already spoken in our chapter on the Uses of Shells. They are among the commonest of our testaceous ornaments, and are remarkable, especially the foreign kinds, for richness and diversity of colour, and the high polish which they bear. The native species are small plain shells, commonly called Pigs, from some real or fancied resemblance which they bear to the swine. They are pretty little white-ribbed shells, and are tolerably plentiful on various parts of the British coasts. There are three kinds— namely, the Louse Pig or Nun Cowry, the Flesh-coloured, and European Pig Cowries. The first of these is of a pale reddish colour, with six square black spots on the back; the second is a beautiful rose tint; and the third is ash-coloured or pinkish, with three black dots and a white streak down the back. The Money Cowry (*Cypræa moneta*), used as current coin in many parts of India, as well as on the coast of Guinea, is a yellow and white shell, with a single band of the former colour; it is small of size, and is sometimes called the Trussed Chicken, for the same reason as the term Pigs is applied to its British relatives. These

Cowries are obtained principally about the Philippine Islands, the Maldive Islands, and the coast of Congo, where, after high tides, the women collect them in baskets, mixed with sand, from which they are afterwards separated and cleaned, when they are ready for the market.

They are only useful as coin so long as they remain unbroken. The value of a single shell is

very small, as the following table will show :— Four Cowries make one gunder; twenty Gunders one punn; four Punns one anna; four Annas one cahaun; and four Cahauns one rupee. The value of the latter coin is equal to two shillings and threepence, English money, and this would be exchangeable for five thousand one hundred and twenty Cowries; so that it would never do to pay large sums in this kind of coin: a waggon would be required to convey a few pounds with. In this country the Money Cowries are frequently used as markers or counters in social games; they are generally white, in shape rather broad and flat, being much spread out round the edges, which are slightly puckered like frills. Here are two figures of the shell, exhibiting the back and front view.

On Plate VII. will be found a group of other Foreign Cowries, most of which will be recognized as familiar ornaments of the mantle and sideboard. Fig. 1 is the Spotted or Leopard Cowry, sometimes also called the Tiger Cowry (*C. tigris*), which, in the earlier stages of its growth, is simply marked with broad bands of lighter colour across the shell. Fig. 2, the Map Cowry (*C. mappa*), curiously marked and shaded so as to resemble a coloured map; there are several varieties of this beautiful shell, such as the rosy and dark variety from the Pearl Islands in the Indian Ocean; the Citron and Dwarf Rich-mouthed variety, from the Mauritius. Fig. 3, the Mole Cowry (*C. talpa*), the last word being the Latin for a mole, is of a more slender form than most other species of the *Cypræidæ* family, so called on account of their beauty—*Cyprea* being a name of Venus, the goddess of beauty. Any one who has seen a mole, must be struck with the resemblance of its general outline to this shell, of which there is a darker-coloured variety of

somewhat stouter form, called *exustus*—burned or
scorched. Of the Poached-egg Cowries there are
several species, the most common is called by
naturalists *Ovulum ovum,* Fig. 4, from *ovum*—an
egg; the back of this shell is much elevated and
rounded; it is smooth and white; the inside is
orange brown. Some of the Poached-egg group
are of a more slender and angular shape, as, for
instance, that called the Gibbous (*O. Gibbosa*); the
moon when more than half-full, is called gibbous—
that is, rounded unequally, as this shell.

 Few shells undergo greater changes,
both of shape and colour, during the
process of growth, than the Cowries,
which are called in France Porcelaines,
on account of their high polish and
brilliant hues; a single species in different stages of development might well be, and
often is, taken for distinct shells. Much might be
said about the Mollusks which inhabit them, but
our present subject has rather to do with their outer
covering than their internal structure. The most
rare and valuable, if not the most beautiful of these
Cowries, is the *C. aurora,* or *aurantium,* Morning-
dawn, or Orange Cowry, a perfect specimen of
which has been sold for fifty guineas. There is a

very curious shell called the Common Weaver's Shuttle (*Oculum volva*), generally included in the *Cyprea* family; of this a representation will be found on Plate VII., Fig. 5. This is brought from China.

# BIVALVES.

ACEPHALOUS MOLLUSKS, with Bivalve Shells, is the name given by modern naturalists to the class of animals of which we have now to speak; the only one of these terms which will require explanation is the first; it comes from the Greek, and means headless, so an Acephalan is a molluscous animal without a head, as

## THE OYSTER,

Which may be considered as the King of Bivalves; his palace, to be sure, is somewhat rough and rugged outside, but within, its walls are smooth and polished, lustrous and iridescent, and altogether beautiful; of a nacrous or pearly appearance, now flushing into a rose tint, now fading into a pure white, and adorned sometimes with goodly pearls of price; truly this monarch of the *Conchifers* has a habitation worthy of a prince, wherein he lives in right royal state. Our readers may smile, perhaps, at the idea of the solitary Oyster doing this, down there on his mud bank or rocky anchorage ground, shut up in his dirty-looking shells, and holding, as it seems, commune with no one, not even his fellow-mollusks; how can he be said to live in royal state, or, indeed, any state at all, except in a most weary, stale, flat, and unprofitable one? And this only shows how erroneously those often judge who do so hastily, and from first appearances.

If we take a peep through a microscope, under the direction of a naturalist named Rymer Jones, we shall see that "the shell of an Oyster is a world occupied by an innumerable quantity of animals, compared to which the Oyster itself is a colossus. The liquid enclosed between the shell of the Oyster contains a multitude of embryos, covered with transparent scales, which swim with ease; a hundred and twenty of these embryos, placed side by side, would make an inch in breadth. This liquid contains besides, a great variety of animalculæ, five hundred times less in size, which give out a phosphoric light. Yet these are not the only inhabitants of this dwelling—there are also three distinct species of worms."

Let us see if there are any hard names here that want explaining before we go any further. The first we stumble upon is *Colossus,* which comes from the Latin, and means a great image or statue, like that which ancient historians tell us once bestrode the entrance to the harbour of Rhodes. *Embryo* comes from the Greek, and means something small and unfinished, that is to expand or grow into a more perfect form, as the seed into a plant. *Animalculæ,* are minute or very small animals, such as cannot be distinguished without the help of a microscope, hence they are sometimes called microscopic animals; this word comes from the Latin *animalis,* which means having life. *Phosphoric* signifies luminous, or giving out light. The Greek name of the morning star is *Phospha.* In Latin, *Phosphorus* is a term applied to a substance which chemists extract from bones and other animal matter, and which, when exposed to air, burns with a pale blue light, like that emitted by the glow-worm. Many of the oceanic or sea animalculæ are exceedingly phosphorescent, so that by night the waves appear like billows of flame. Of this luminosity of the ocean, as it is termed, we shall have to speak on another occasion. We will now return to the Oyster, who, it will be seen, is by no means so solitary in his bivalve palace as might be supposed. He has his torch-bearers, and other attendants,

quite a host of them, no doubt magnificently dressed, if we could but see them to advantage, and well instructed in the several duties which they have to perform. Oh yes, certainly, as the Irish poet has said,

> " Of all the Conchiferous shell-fish,
> The Oyster *is* surely the King."

Shall we continue the quotation ? and say

> " Arrah Mick, call the people who sell fish,
> And tell them a dozen to bring;
> For it's I that intend to demonstrate,
> The creature's phenomena strange,
> Its functions to set every one straight,
> And exhibit their structure and range."

Scarcely will our limited space permit us to do this, but a few of the most remarkable particulars about this common Acephalan, we feel called upon to set before our readers.

First, then, it belongs to the class *Conchifera.* This is a word which we must stop to examine a little; it seems to come from the Latin *concha,* which means a shell-fish with two shells—in other words, a bivalve mollusk. Second, our Oyster belongs to the class *Pectinidæ.* Now *pecten* is the Latin for a comb, and this class includes those

bivalve shells whose edges are toothed, or, as it is
said, *pectinated.* In the scallop and the cockle shells
this peculiarity is more observable than in those of
other members of the class, and these form the
typical, or, so to speak, pattern genus, *pecten.*
Thirdly, the Common Oyster is a *Monomyarian
Conchifer.* Ah! that's something like a name for
the acephaloid monarch! Look at these two words,
*mono-myarian, di-myarian.* You know, of course,
that mony-syllable means one syllable, and dis-
syllable means two. You sometimes hear of a
person who leads a *monotonous* life, and you think,
perhaps, of the Oyster shut up in his shell all alone,
*one* by himself. This notion you now know to be a
false one, although it is true that he has but one
abductor muscle, and therefore belongs to the
division of the *Pectinidæ* family called *Monomyaria,*
while the Pearl Oyster has two, and therefore
belongs to that termed *Dimyaria.* If, as they say,
there is reason in the roasting of eggs, surely there
must be in the names given to the classes and
divisions of shells. We hope to have succeeded in
making the why and the wherefore in this case
somewhat plain; *one—two—*and away we go out of
this maze of hard names. But what about the
abductor muscle, above spoken of? Well, this

must be explained; *abduce,* coming from the Latin *abduco,* means to separate, to draw away. Hence we have *abduction.* During the life of an Oyster, the usual and natural state of the shell is that of being kept open for a little distance, to allow the water necessary for its nourishment and respiration to flow in and out; but as a security against danger, it was necessary to furnish the animal with the means of rapidly closing the shell, and retaining the valves in a closed state. These actions being only occasional, yet requiring considerable force, are effected by means of a muscular power, for which purpose one or two, or sometimes more, strong muscles are placed between the valves, their fibres passing directly across from the inner surface of one to that of the other, and firmly attached to both; and these are called the abductor muscles, because their office is to draw or pull. How strongly they do this, those whose business it is to open Oysters can best tell. If the animal within were not alive, the process would not be a difficult one, as in that case the muscles would be relaxed, and the shell would come open of itself, so that actually people who eat Oysters directly they are opened, swallow them "all alive-O!"

If a pair of the shells from which the delicious

morsel has been extracted be taken in the hand, it
may be noticed that one is much thinner, smoother,
and flatter than the other: this is the side most
exposed to the action of the water; the rougher
and rounder side is that which is attached to the
rock or other substance to which the animal forms
an attachment that is usually life-long.  The two
portions of the shell are joined together by a hinge
of curious workmanship, which is formed of the
inner layer of the shell, and strengthened by a
ligament which is wonderfully elastic; when the
shell is drawn together by the abductor muscles, the
ligament is at full stretch, and as soon as they relax
at all, it contracts, and causes the shell to gape.
This process is repeated as often as may be necessary for the safety and sustenance of the animal
within, whose mouth is situated at the narrowest
part of its habitation—namely, near the joint of the
hinge which connects its upper and under shell.  The
anatomical structure of the Oyster is more perfect
than would be supposed, from its apparently low
state of organization; it has a heart, liver, and in-
testinal canal, and a bag near the mouth, which
answers the purpose of a stomach.  Its breathing
organs are gills, closely resembling those of most
other fish; it has little vessels which convey the

bile from the stomach to the liver, and may, perhaps, be subject to bilious attacks as well as those who swallow this curious piece of organization at a mouthful, without thinking at all of the goodly structure they are demolishing. There is the tiny heart with its series of blood-vessels, just as perfect as in the larger animals. There are the nerves in the shape of minute feelers, which appear to be acutely sensible not only of actual contact with foreign bodies, but also of sounds and movements from without. A very nice sense of feeling appears to reside in what is called the beard, in scientific language *bissus;* this is a kind of double fringe to the two lobes of the mantle, or sac, as it is called, which envelops the body of the animal, and floats free from the shell, except just at the part nearer the valve where it is attached.

We have just spoken of the beard of the Oyster, and this reminds us of a conundrum which may serve to amuse our readers, and enliven these dry details a little. Why is an Oyster the most anomalous—that is strange, contradictory—creature in existence? Do you give it up? Well, then, it is because

"It wears a beard without any chin,
And leaves its bed to be tucked in."

Again, by this allusion to the "tucking in" of Oysters, a phrase more expressive than polite, we have recalled to memory the saying of a quaint old uthor, that they are "ungodly, uncharitable, and unprofitable meat: ungodly, because they are eaten without grace; uncharitable, because they leave nothing but shells; and unprofitable, because they must swim in wine." Not, generally, however, are they eaten in this luxurious manner; a little pepper and vinegar is all that they commonly get in the way of sauce, and those who swallow them thus accompanied, seem to do so with infinite relish. A very long chapter, if not a whole book, might be written about the historical associations of Oysters, for which our country has been famous, as far back as the time of the first Roman invasion; much, too, might be said about the Oyster beds and fisheries, which give employment to thousands of our industrious population; but all this has so little to do with natural history, that we can find no excuse for dwelling upon it here. It is quite within the range of our subject, however, to state that the "spat" or "spawn" of the Oyster is cast about the beginning of May: at first it resembles a drop of greenish tallow, but by the aid of the microscope it may be seen to consist of a great number of minute parti-

cles, each of which is an egg, and will by and by
become a perfect fish; these increase in size very
rapidly, and after floating about for a while, sink to
the bottom, and become attached to rock or some
other substance, in which position, if not violently
detached or removed, they complete their growth and
live out the term of their natural life. Their food
minute animalculæ, and microscopic vegetation, on
the nature of which their flavour greatly depends.

They have many enemies besides man; the
whelk, and the crab, the sea-star or "five fingers,"
and the large drum-fish, which swallows them
almost by the bushel, shells and all; these help to
thin the Oyster-beds, and make the dredger's

labours less remunerative than they would otherwise be. Here is a picture of one as he stands in

his boat just about to throw his dredge into the sandy bottom, where he knows the delicious testaceans do, or ought to, lie most thickly. The dredge, which is a triangular iron frame with a net over the bottom, will naturally sink, and when the line to which it is attached ceases to run out, the dredger will put his boat in motion, and draw it thus over the Oyster-bed, and then pull it up filled, it may be, with little fat " Miltons," or large " Colchesters," or such other kind as the spot is known to yield.

The Latin for Oyster is *Ostrea,* and that is a name given to a genus of the *Pectinidæ* family, comprising beside the *O. edulis,* or common Oyster, many other species. *Edulis* means eatable. Some naturalists divide these Ostraceans into two groups, first with simple or undulated, but not plaited valves; second, those which have the borders of their valves distinctly plaited.

To the first group belong the Common Oyster, and between thirty and forty other living species, which are found principally in warm and temperate latitudes. In the Polar ocean none have been discovered, and in the hotter climates they are most abundant, being found in large beds or banks near the coast, and often attached to rocks, and even to trees which grow by the water, so that the accounts of some old travellers who stated that they saw Oysters growing upon trees, were not so false as many supposed them.

The annexed figure is that of the Cock's-comb

Oyster, *Ostrea Crista-Galli,* a native of the Indian Seas, and a very remarkable shell, on account of its crooked or deeply indented form; the specific name

means cock's-crest. The Chinese Window Oyster, called *Placuna Placenta,* which we may, if we like, translate into a pleasant or agreeable cake, the shell, it will be seen, is round like a cake, and its smoothness and regularity of form render it agreeable to look upon. This species, too, comes from the Indian Seas, where it is taken on sandy bottoms. The American Spiny Oyster, or *Spondylus Americanus,* brings us into another family, that of the Water Clams, called by naturalists *Spondylidæ;*

with the spines stuck out every way, and no way in particular, it looks like a head of hair greatly in need of the assistance of one of its *pectinated* relatives. The specific name of this curious shell explains itself; the generic name comes from the Latin *Spondylis*—a kind of serpent.

Passing over the family *Malleidæ,* or Hammer Oysters, we come to the *Meleagrinidæ,* or Pearl Oysters, of which Fig. 1, Plate VIII. is an example.

This is the *M. Margaritifera* of naturalists, the mollusk in whose shells pearls are chiefly found. Here are two long words; *Meleagris* is the Latin for a Guinea or Turkey Hen, to the markings of whose plumage naturalists might have imagined the shells of this genus bore some resemblance. There was, says the mythology, a celebrated hero of antiquity named Meleaga, but we can hardly suppose that there is any association between his name and that of a genus of Oysters, of which edible we read the ancients were very fond, and they are said to have had a fancy, not only for the mollusk itself, but also for the pearls found in its shell, which at their luxurious banquets they dissolved in wine, to make the draughts richer, or, at all events, more expensive; and this brings us to the specific name of the Pearl Oyster, *Margaritifera*, which comes from the Latin *Margarita*—a pearl; the French use this word slightly altered in the spelling (thus, *Marguerite*) for both a daisy and

## A PEARL.

This jewel, so highly valued for its chaste beauty, is but a secretion of animal matter, resulting from the efforts of some uneasy mollusk, annoyed by a foreign substance, which has found its way into his habitation, to make the best of an unavoidable evil by enclosing it in a soft smooth covering. Let us imitate the Oyster; and when annoyed or afflicted, by meekness and patience, and Christian charity, strive to turn our vexations and troubles into "pearls of great price," and "goodly pearls," like those mentioned in Scripture.

It is on the north-west coast of the Island of Ceylon, in the Indian Ocean, that the Pearl Oyster most abounds, and there it is that the Pearl fishery is conducted in the most extensive, systematic, and successful manner; this fishing commences at the beginning of March, and upwards of two hundred boats are usually employed in it; in each of these boats are ten divers, who go down to the Oyster-beds, five at a time, and so relieve each other; there are besides thirteen other men who manage the boat and attend to the divers. Altogether, it is computed that from fifty to sixty thousand persons, in some way engaged in the fishery, or preparation, or sale of the pearls, assemble at and near the scene of operations, which must be indeed a busy one. The number of Oysters taken during the period of the fishing, which is about a month, must be prodigious. One boat has been known to bring on shore, in the day, as many as thirty-three thousand; they are placed in heaps, and allowed to remain until they become putrid, when they undergo a very elaborate process of washing and separating from the shells, which are carefully examined and deprived of their pearly treasures. The stench arising from the decomposed animal matter is described as horrible, and the whole process filthy and loathsome in the extreme; yet out of the slime and mud and disgusting effluvia, come every year gems of inestimable value, calculated to adorn the brow of beauty and form ornaments the most pure and delicate that can be imagined. For the exclusive right of fishing on the banks of Ceylon for a single season, as much as £120,000 have been paid to the English Government by one person, who sublets boats to others. Pearls vary greatly in value according to their colour and size; those which are perfectly white are the most valuable; next to these are those which have a yellowish tinge; the smallest kind, used for various ornamental purposes, are called seed pearls, the refuse is made into a kind of confection called *chimum*, highly relished by Chinese epicures. A single oyster will sometimes contain several pearls, which are generally embedded in the body of the animal, but are sometimes fixed to the shell; it is recorded of one rich mollusk, that there were found in his possession no less than one hundred and fifty precious jewels; he must have been a miser, or perhaps he had taken them in pledge from his less provident neighbours.

From the earliest time, pearls have been considered as valuable ornaments; they are mentioned in the book of Job (see chap. xxviii. verse 18), and are often alluded to by Greek and Roman writers. Various attempts have been made to imitate them, and one mode of producing them, practised, it is said, more than a thousand years ago, is still carried on in China. In the shells of Pearl Oysters, holes are bored, into which pieces of iron are introduced; these wounding and irritating the animal, cause it to deposit coat upon coat of pearly matter over the wounded part, and so the pearl is formed. Artificial pearls are made of hollow glass globules or little globes, covered on the inside with a liquid called pearl-essence, and filled up with white wax. Historians speak of an ancient traffic in native pearls carried on by this country; and in modern times, British pearls of considerable value have been discovered—one not many years since, by a gentleman who was eating oysters at Winchester, was valued at two hundred guineas. Generally the pearls of this country are inferior in the two requisites of colour and size.

Interesting accounts of Pearls and Pearl-fishing, will be found in "The Penny" and "Saturday Magazines," and many other works easy of access. There our young readers may learn of the perils and dangers to which the poor divers are exposed from the voracious sharks, which hover about the fishing grounds, and make a dash at their victim, heedless of the written charms with which the priest or shark-charmer has provided him previous to his descent, and of much more than we can find space here to tell. All we can now do is to give the portrait, as drawn by Thomas Hood, of a lady who takes up her abode in all the pearl-producing bivalves, and who is, therefore, perhaps on this account, called

MOTHER OF PEARL.

## THE MUSSEL AND THE COCKLE.

It is in the *Dimyaria* division of the *Conchifera* that we must look for those familiar bivalves, the Mussel, or, as it is sometimes spelled, Muscle, and the Cockle; the former, called in scientific language *Mytilus*, which in Latin means simply a shell-fish; and the latter *Cardium*, which may have reference to the hinge of this bivalve, or the heart-shape assumed by several of the species; *cardo*, in Latin, signifying the hinge of a gate, and *cardesco*, a stone in the shape of a heart.

It is to the *Mytilidæ* family that we shall first direct our attention; and here we find the Common or Edible Mussel (*M. edule*), and many other species, in all of which the shell is more or less elongated or lengthened out, and pointed at one end. The members of this family are abundant on most rocky coasts, where facilities are afforded for the mollusks to moor themselves to rocks, stones, and other substances covered at high-water, but left dry by the retreating tide. They are not, however, confined to shores of this description, but are sometimes found in vast numbers on low sandy or pebbly flats, which run far out into the sea; these are called beds of Mussels, and are, like the Oyster

grounds, specially cared for and protected. As a ship by its cable, so commonly the Mussel, by its bissus or beard, is made fast to its anchorage-ground, be it pebbly or sandy beach, or jutting rock. Sometimes, however, the mollusk travels; and this is how it manages to do so : it has a stout, fleshy foot, in shape something like that of a chubby child, and this it can advance about two inches beyond the edge of the shell, then fixing the point of it to a piece of rock or any other body, and contracting it, the shell is drawn onward, and sure, though slow, progress is made in any desired direction. The *Pinna,* as the marine Mussel is called, has a foot which is cylindrical in shape, and has at the bottom a round tendon, almost as long as itself, the use of which appears to be to gather in and retain the numerous threads with which, when inhabiting the shores of tempestuous seas, it lashes itself fast to the fixed objects around; these threads are fastened at various points, and then drawn tight by the animal, whose instinct teaches it that its brittle shell would soon be broken in pieces, if suffered to roll hither and thither at the mercy of the waves.

The Mussel has a very curious method of preparing its cable for this service; it is not woven,

7

nor spun, nor drawn out of the body, like the web
of the spider, but produced in a liquid form, and
cast in a mould which is formed by a groove in
the foot, extending from the root of the tendon to
the upper extremity; the sides of this groove are
formed so as to fold over it and form a canal, into
which the glutinous or sticky secretion is poured;
there it remains until it has dried into a solid
thread, when the end of it is carried out by the
foot, and applied to the object to which it is to be
attached; the canal is then opened through its
whole length to free the thread, and closing again
is ready for another casting; as if conscious how
much depends upon the security of his lines, the
animal tries every one after he has fixed it by
swinging itself round so as to put the threads
fully on the stretch. When once they are firmly
fixed, it seems to have no power of disengaging
itself from them; the liquid matter out of which
they are formed is so very glutinous, or glue-like,
as to attach itself firmly to the smoothest bodies.
The process of producing it is a slow one, as it
does not appear that the *Pinna* can form more than
four or five in the course of twenty-four hours.
When the animal is disturbed in its operations, it
sometimes forms these threads too hastily; they

are then more slender than those produced at leisure, and, of a consequence, weaker. On some parts of the Mediterranean coast, as in Sicily, gloves and other articles have been manufactured from the threads of this mollusk. They resemble very fine silk in appearance.

The foot of the Cockle, of which we here give a figure, is commonly employed in scooping out the mud or sand, beneath which it  conceals itself; this useful limb assumes the form of a shovel, hook, or any other instrument necessary for the purpose; it appears to be a mass of muscular fibres, and to possess great power. As a boatman in shallow water sends his vessel along by pushing against the bottom with his boat-hook, precisely so does *Mr. Cardium* travel; he doubles up his foot into a club, and by an energetic use of it as a propeller, makes considerable headway along the surface of the soft sand beneath the waters. In this way, too, some members of the genus *solen* force their way through the sand; while those called *Tellina* spring to a considerable distance, by first folding the foot into a small compass, and then suddenly expanding it, closing the shell at the same time with a loud snap ; so that you see these sober-looking mollusks are sometimes frolicsome fellows : this is an enforcement of the lesson, judge not by appearances.

Some of the species, both of the Mussel and Cockle families, have very beautiful shells. We give a representation of one of each, on Plate VIII. Fig. 2 is the Magellanic Mytilus, (*M. Magellanicus,*) found chiefly in the Straits of Magellan ; it is generally four or five inches long; the shells when polished are very brilliant, the deep purple colour changing into rich violet, as they are held in different lights. In most cabinets the large fan-like delicate shells of the genus *Pinna* may be observed; the largest species is that called *Pinna flabellum*, taken in the Mediterranean; it sometimes exceeds two feet in length. The first of these names is a Latin word signifying, besides a shell-fish, the fin of a fish, or the wing-feathers of a bird —hence the term pinion ; it refers to the fin-like or wing-like shape of this shell. *Flabellum* means a fan, referring probably to the bissus of the mollusk, which is fine and glossy, like silk, and very abundant.

Many pretty specimens for figuring might be selected from the *Naidæ*, a family of Fresh-water

Mussels, so called from the Naiades, fabulous divinities of the streams and rivers. The shells of many of these, which are of considerable thickness, are lined with the most brilliant nacre, and in these, as might be expected, pearls are sometimes found. One species, abundant in some English rivers, called the *Mya Margaritifera,* or, as some say, *Uno elongates,* has long been celebrated for this valuable production. It was most likely with pearls from this mollusk that Julius Cæsar adorned a breast-plate, which he dedicated to Venus, and hung up in her temple. The rivers Esk and Conway were formerly celebrated as British pearl fishing-grounds; a Conway pearl was presented by her chamberlain, Sir Richard Wynn, of Gwyder, to Catherine, Queen of Charles the Second; and in the royal crown of Britain this jewel is said still to occupy a place. Sir John Hawkins, the circumnavigator of the globe, held a patent for the pearl-fishery of the River Irt, in Cumberland. The rivers of Tyrone and Donegal, in Ireland, have, or had, their pearl-bearing Mussels; we read of one which weighed thirty-six carats (a carat is nearly four grains), but not being of perfect shape and colour, it was only valued at forty pounds. We also read of another purchased by Lady Glenlealy, for ten pounds, and found to be so perfect and admirable, that eighty pounds was afterwards offered for it, and refused.

These *Naidœ* have not a bissus like the Marine Mussels, they are therefore never attached to one object; they use their foot as a propeller in traversing the muddy floor of the pond or river, and they have a very funny way of getting along indeed; first, they open the valves of the shell, put out the foot, and, after some little hard work, manage to set themselves up on edge; they then proceed by a series of jerks, leaving a deepish furrow in the mud behind them.

We will now go to Fig. 3, the Spined Cytherea, the *Cytherea*, or *Venus Dione* of naturalists; the meaning of the term is the mother of Venus, who was, as you will remember, the goddess of beauty, given to this shell, perhaps, because it is entitled to occupy a place at the head of the *Cytherea*, a genus of the *Cardiidœ*, or Cockle family, of which genus there are about seventy-eight living species; this, as it is the most rare, is also, perhaps, the most beautiful; it is found in the seas of America, and is remarkable for the row of spines on the hinder border of each valve; these vary much in size and number, being in some individuals long and far apart, in others, short, thick, and closely set. The colour of the shell also varies considerably, being sometimes of a delicate rose colour ; at others, more of a claret ; at others again bordering on purple. It was for one of the first discovered specimens of this shell that £1000 is said to have been given. Truly a Venus of value this ; it ought to be called the Queen of Cockles !

Our next examples (see Fig. 4), is the Spotted Tridacna (*T. maculatus*), the latter term signifying spotted. In the *Chamidæ*, or Clam family, is placed the *Tridacna* genus, the discovered species of which are not numerous ; they are chiefly found in the Indian seas. The one above-mentioned claims pre-eminence for beauty. We cannot quite see the applicability of the generic name ; *Tridacnus*, in Latin, signifies to be eaten at three bites, but he must be a man of large capacity indeed who could so devour the head of this family, the Giant Tridacna (*T. gigas*), a single specimen of which has been known to weigh as much as five hundred and seventy pounds ; from three to four hundred is by no means an uncommon size. The shell of this giant mollusk is of a very picturesque shape, something like its spotted *congener* (as we call anything of the same kind or genus), only it is somewhat plainer, and more deeply ribbed and indented. The

inside is of a glossy whiteness, and it is frequently
used as a basin for garden fountains, or the reception
of rills or little jets of water, which sparkle in its
stainless hollow. In the church of St. Salpice, at
Paris, is a shell of this immense Clam, the valves of
which are used as receptacles for holy water; it
was presented to Francis the First by the republic
of Venice. Fancy the clapping to of such a pair of
valves when the animal closes its shell in alarm, and

the strength of the cable required to moor it to the
rocks or coral reef. The spotted species here
figured has a solid and heavy shell, very elegantly
shaped, and beautifully marked, as will be seen;
the greatly reduced size of the figure prevents anything like justice being done to the original.

The above is a figure of the Heart Isocardea

(*I. cor*), which is also a member of the Clam family, and one of the most elegantly-shaped shells in the whole range of Conchology. It is a native of the Mediterranean and other seas of Europe, and has been taken in deep water on the west coast of Ireland. We complete this group with a representation of the curious *Arcadæ* family, or Ark shells,

as they are commonly called, because one of the species was thought to resemble the ark built by Noah. Mr. Swainson tells us that the animals of these shells affix themselves to other bodies by a particular muscle, which is protruded through the gaping part of the valves; they also adhere, when young, by means of the bissiform epidermis, or bissus-like outer skin: this species is a native of the Atlantic Ocean and the seas of Europe. The Antique Ark (*A. antiqua*) is very like the Common Cockle, being of a white colour, and heart-shaped.

We here give a representation of this shell, and also of the shell of the pretty little Pearly Trigonia (*T. margaritacea*), included in the *Arcadæ* family; this is a rare species, found only in the seas of New Holland.

———

## SCALLOP SHELLS.

Several species of Scallop Shells are found scattered about on our shores; they belong, as before stated, to the family *Pectinidæ*, the meaning of which term has been already explained. These shells were called by Cuvier " the Butterflies of the Ocean," on account of the various and beautiful colours which they exhibit. Some of them are exceedingly thin, and brittle as glass; one species found in the Arctic regions is as transparent as that substance, and is therefore called *P. vitreus*, from the Latin for glass, which is *vitreum*. One of the commonest of our native Scallops is the St. James's Cockle (*P. Jacobæus*). This shell is found in great plenty along our southern coasts; it is often referred to by old writers, on account of having been commonly worn in the hats of pilgrims to Palestine or the Holy

Land, as the scene of our Saviour's life and death
was called. Sir Walter Raleigh, in his poem called
"The Pilgrimage," thus enumerates the different
articles considered necessary for a Palmer, as these
pilgrims were termed :—

"Give me my *scallop shell* of quiet,
   My *staff* of faith to lean upon,
My *scrip* of joy (immortal diet),
   My *bottle* of salvation,
My *gown* of glory, hope's true gage,
   And thus I'll make my pilgrimage."

This mollusk, it may be noticed, like many other
bivalves, has a flat and a concave or hollow shell.
In early times, when plates and drinking vessels
were not so plentiful as they are now, one of these
served the former purpose, and the other the latter.
Thus, in speaking of a feast, a Gaelic or Scottish
bard has said—

"The joy of the *shell* went round."

Sometimes the species termed *Pecten opercularis* was
used as the pilgrim's badge : the specific name comes
most likely from the Latin *operculum*, whose meaning
has been explained.

This, too, is a common British shell, as is also
the little speckled Scallop (*P. varia*), which may be

found on almost any part of the coast where the water-line is margined with a sandy ridge. The shells are generally about two inches long, of various

COMMON SCALLOP.

colours, clouded, speckled, and marked with about twelve ribs. There is a foreign species called the Flounder Scallop (*P. pleuronectes*), which is remarkable for having the two valves of the shell of different colours, the upper one being of a rich reddish brown, and the lower one white. The specific name has reference to this, being compounded of the Latin *pleura,* something double, and *necto,* to join. The fish called the Flounder is brown above and white beneath; hence the English name of this shell. The preceding engraving of the Common Scallop, viewed from the front, shows the flat and concave form of the two valves of this shell, and also the depth of the indentations or ridges.

———

### LIMPETS.

Among the rocks of the British coast there are no shells more frequently met with than those of the Common Limpet (*Patella vulgata*); they lie scattered about like so many little empty cups, each having, on the death of the molluks, fallen from the rocky cavity in which it was embedded, and which was just large enough to contain it. Here the animal attaches itself so firmly by its fibrous foot, which is hollow in the centre, and acts like a sucker, that it is almost impossible to loosen its hold otherwise than by inserting something thin, like the blade of a knife, between it and the stone. By this power of adhesion, the Limpet is protected from the violence of the waves, and also from its numerous enemies, aquatic birds and animals, which have a relish for its flesh. Still vast numbers are used as food, both by man and the inferior creatures, so that the means of defence furnished to the Limpets of the rock are not always sure. "The peasantry of the western isles of Scotland," we are told by Miss Pratt, "look to the Periwinkles and Limpets, which abound on the rocks, for their daily meal, often for long seasons subsisting almost entirely upon this humble food. In the Isle of Skye, the inhabitants are often, at one time of the year, without any other source of provision." Then comes the Sea-gull, and the Duck, and the Pied Oyster-catcher, to feed on the poor little mollusk, the bill of the latter bird being admirably adapted for loosening its hold on the rock.

*Patella* in Latin signifies a salad-dish, a knee-pan, and several other domestic utensils, of a broad shallow make; and hence we find the plural form of the word applied to the Limpet family, whose shells are of such a shape. Members of this family are found on all rocky coasts, except those of the Arctic seas; on tropical rocks they grow to a large size, and form a valuable article of food. A very curious piece of mechanism is the tongue of the Common Limpet; it is from two to three inches long, and has a spoon-like extremity, so that it looks, when extended from the mouth, like a small snake. If examined through a microscope, it is seen to be armed throughout its whole extent with rows, four deep, of sharp hooked teeth, and between each row are placed two others, which have three points, and are set in a slanting position. The use of this arrangement we cannot at present determine, but no doubt it has a perfect adaptation to the wants of the animal.

There are shell-fish called Key-hole Limpets, which belong to the genus *Fissurellidæ*, from *fissura*, a cleft or slip, from whence comes also fissure. All the members of this genus are distinguished by the aperture at the top of the shell, shaped like a key-hole, which is situated exactly over the breathing organs, and serves as a channel for the water necessary for respiration.

Frequently upon the fronds of the large olive sea-weeds may be found a tiny shell shaped something like that of the Common Limpet. It is of an olive-green colour, with blue streaks, and is called, from its clearness, the Pellucid Limpet (*P. pellucida*). There is also another much like it in appearance, which naturalists call *P. lœvis*. To the labours of these little mollusks, according to Dr. Harvey, may be attributed the destruction of the gigantic Algæ (sea-weed). Eating into the lower part of the stems, and destroying the branches of the roots, they so far weaken the base that it becomes unable to support the weight of the frond, and thus the plant is detached and driven on shore by the waves.

"And so the forest tall, that groweth
  Underneath the waters clear,
Does the little woodman mollusk
  Level every year;
From small causes, great results—
  Teaching you to persevere."

## ROCK-BORERS.

The family *Pholadæ* comprises a group of mollusks, the boring habits of which have long been known; they penetrate wood, hard clay, chalk, and rocks, and devastate the labours of man; they attack the hulls of ships, the piles which form the foundations of piers and breakwaters, and they force themselves upon our attention by the loss of property, as well as life, which results from their hidden depredations. Of this family, those belonging to the genus *Pholas* may be more especially likened to the Edomites of Scripture, because they take up their abode in the rock, and hollow out for themselves dwellings therein. With a shell as thin as paper, and brittle as glass, the wonder is how

these Rock-borers work their way into and through
hard stones. Some naturalists assert that they
effect this by means of an acid which decomposes
the substance of the rock, and renders it soft;
others, that the animal keeps turning round and
round like an instrument called an auger, and so
gradually rasps away the surface of the stone with
the angles of its shell, but we question whether
the shell would not be worn out first in such a process. The generic name of these " stone-piercers,"
comes from the Greek word *Pholeo*—to hide, and
the rocky chambers which they hollow out for themselves, are as snug hiding-places as can well be
imagined; yet however deep they may go into
these gloomy caverns, as we should be apt to
suppose them, they need not be in darkness; for it
appears that these Pholades emit a most remarkable
light—whether phosphorescent or not does not
appear to be determined; so strong is it, that it is
said to illuminate the mouth of the person who eats
the mollusk; and it is remarked by Dr. Priestly,
that " contrary to the nature of most fish, which
give light when they tend to putrescence, this is
more luminous the fresher it is, and when dried its
light will revive on being moistened with water."
So that in more respects than one these Rock-borers

8

are mysteries. The most common of them, perhaps, is the Prickly Pidduck, or Peckstone (*P. dactylus*), which is much used by the fishermen of our coasts as bait; the specific name is the Latin for a fruit shaped like a finger, which is something like the shape of this mollusk, as will be seen by the annexed engraving.

The genus *Pholus* is very widely distributed, and all the species have the same boring habits as those of our own coast, which we need not enumerate. Like them, too, in this respect, are the marine worms called *Teredo,* which make their way into the bottoms of ships, and all submerged timber, but these will be more fully spoken of in another volume. The above figure exhibits the *Pholas dactylus* as it appears in a section of rock, split open for the purpose of seeing the shelly miner at his work.

# MULTIVALVES.

WE have insensibly passed from the Bivalve shells to those composed of several pieces, and therefore called Multivalves; probably, perhaps, the Rock-borers, last described, come into this division, for although their covering consists mainly of two principal portions or valves, yet there are often additional parts; in some a calcareous tube envelops the whole mollusk, leaving only an opening behind. This is more especially the case with those which most resemble worms, such as the genera *Teredina* and *Teredo,* included by Lamarck in the family which he calls *Tubulidæ.*

The first group of multivalves we shall have to notice, are

## THE CHITONS,

forming the family *Chitonidæ.* The term has a Greek derivation, and means a coat of mail. These mollusks are covered by a shell formed of eight distinct portions, arranged along the back in a single row, and attached to a mantle which re-

resembles leather, being very tough and wrinkled; the edges of this mantle extend beyond the borders of the plates, which overlap each other, so as to constitute a kind of armour, very different from the conical shell of the Limpet, or the turbinated, that is twisted, case of some of the Borers. The coverings of the Chitons are variously marked, so that each distinct species is known by its peculiar pattern, as a knight of old by the quarterings of his shield. All the mantles, however, have scaly, hairy, or spiny margins. In this coat of mail the animal can roll itself up like an armadillo, and so be tolerably secure from its enemies; it has an oval foot, the sides of which are covered with small leaflets, and by means of this it can attach itself to rocks, like the Limpet, or travel about in search of adventures. It has no distinct head, therefore it is *acephalous;* nor any perceptible eyes. The mouth is furnished with a long tongue, curled up spirally, like a watch-spring, and armed with horny teeth.

The members of the Chiton family are numerous, being found on most rocky shores; they attain the largest size in the hottest climates, having never been found very far north. The British species are small, and not more than two or three

in number; they may be found adhering to stones
near low-water mark.  We give
a figure of one of these, called
the Tufted Chiton (*C. fascicu-*
*laris*).  This word is from the
Latin *fasciculus,* a little bundle of leaves or flowers,
and it refers to the hairy tufts that edge the mantle
of this marine slug.

## BARNACLES,

Or, as they are sometimes called, Bernicles, belong
to what naturalists term the class *Cirrhopoda,* sometimes spelled *cirripeda,* which appears to be derived
from the Latin *cirrus*—a tuft or lock of hair curled,
and *pede*—a foot; hence the term may be translated
hairy-footed.  Such of our readers as have seen
the Common or Duck Barnacle (*Pentalasmis anati-*
*fera*) will at once understand the applicability of
this term.  Many a piece of drift-wood comes to
land literally covered with long fleshy stalks, generally of a purplish red colour, twisting and curling
in all directions, and terminating in delicate porce-
lain-like shells, clear and brittle, of a white colour,
just tinged with blue, from between which project
the many-jointed *cirrhi,* or hair-like tentacles, which

serve the purpose of a casting-net, to seize and drag to the mouth of the animal its prey, which consists of small mollusks and crustacea.

This is the Barnacle about which such strange stories are told by old writers, who affirmed that the Barnacle or Brent Goose, that in winter visits our shores, is produced from these fleshy foot-stalks and hairy shells by a natural process of growth, or, as some philosophers of our day would say, of development. Gerard, who, in 1597, wrote a "Historie of Plants," describes the process by which the fish is transformed into the bird; telling his readers that as "the shells gape, the legs hang out, that the bird growing bigger and bigger, the shells open more and more, till at length it is attached only by the bill, soon after which it drops into the sea; there it acquires feathers, and grows to a fowle." There is an amusing illustration given in Gerard's book, where the young Geese are represented hanging on the branches of trees, just ready to drop into the water, where a number of those that have previously fallen, like ripe fruit, and attained their full plumage, are sailing about very contentedly. It was part of this theory that the Barnacles were of vegetable origin, they grew upon trees, or sprung out of the ground like mushrooms; so we find, in the works of an old poet named Du Bartas, these lines:—

" So slow Bootes underneath him sees
In the icy islands goslings hatched of trees,
Whose fruitful leaves, falling into the water,
Are turned, as known, to living fowls soon after;
So rotten planks of broken ships do change
To Barnacles.   O transformation strange!
'Twas first a green tree, then a broken hull,
Lately a mushroom, now a flying gull."

The investigations of modern science have quite exploded this foolish notion; we now know exactly what transformations the Barnacle undergoes; strange enough some of them are, but it does not change into a Goose, although its specific name has reference to that bird, being derived from *anas*, the Latin for Goose.

The shell of the Barnacle is composed of five pieces joined together by membranes; four pieces are lateral, that is to say, they form the sides, the word comes from the Latin *latus*—a side; the other is a single narrow slip, which fills what would otherwise be an open space down the back between the valves; these parts of the shell appear to be somewhat loosely connected, so as to allow free action to the animal lodged within, which is enclosed in a fine skin or mantle. The mouth is placed at the lower part, near the opening, whence the *cirrhi* issue forth; this mouth is a curious piece of mechanism, being furnished with a horny lip covered with minute *palpi*, or feelers; there are three pairs of *mandibles*, that is jaws, the two outer ones being horny and *serrated*, that is jagged or toothed like a saw; the inner one is soft and membranous, that is, composed of little fibres, like strings, crossing each other, as we see what are called the veins in a leaf.

Much more might be said about the internal structure of the Cirrhopods, or *Balani*, as the Barnacle group is sometimes called, from the Latin *Balanus*—a kind of acorn. By some naturalists, the term is not applied to the stalked *Cirrhipoda*, like that we have been describing, but only to the *sessile* kinds, that is, those which set close or grow low; from the same Latin root comes the English word *session*—a settling. The coverings of these Dwarf Barnacles are sometimes called acorn shells; they are commonly white, of an irregular cone shape, composed of several ribbed pieces, closely fitted together with an opening at the top, closed by an *operculum*, or stopper.

These shells cover in patches the surface of

exposed rocks, drift wood, and any other substance. Some of the mollusks affix themselves to the bodies of whales, others form a lodgment in the hollows of corals and sponges. Once fixed they remain so during life, taking their chance of such suitable food as may come within their limited sphere of action. At an earlier stage of their existence, both their shape and habits are very different, being lively little creatures, swimming about hither and thither like water-fleas. They are about the tenth of an inch long, and of most grotesque appearance, having six-jointed legs set with hairs, the whole being so arranged that they act in concert, and striking or flapping the water, send the little body along in a series of bounds; then the creature has two long arms, each furnished with hooks and a sucker, and a tail tipped with bristles, which is usually folded up under the body; its pair of large staring eyes are *pedunculated*, that is, set upon foot-stalks; it has a house on its back, like a bivalve shell, into which it can collect its scattered members when occasion requires. When of sufficient age to settle itself in life, and become a staid member of submarine society, it fixes itself to some convenient object, throws away its eyes as no longer useful, gets rid of its preposterous limbs, enlarges its house, and sits down to fishing in a small way for an honest and respectable livelihood.

A piece of timber covered with Stalked Barnacles, wriggling and twisting about like so many helmeted snakes, and waving their plume-like *cirrhi*, is a very curious sight.   They sometimes

attach themselves to ships' bottoms in such numbers as to retard their progress through the water; they do not, however, bore into and destroy the timber, like the *Teredines*, or ship-worms, to which we have alluded in our brief notice of the *Pholadœ*. The growth of Barnacles must be very rapid, as a ship perfectly free from them, will often return after a short voyage, with her bottom below the water-line completely covered.

We give a representation of a group of these stalked mollusks, as they appear affixed to a piece of timber. This is the Common, or Duck Barnacle.

## CUTTLE-FISH.

Strange and monstrous as are the forms of many of the creatures that inhabit the deep, there are, perhaps, none more so than those belonging to that division of the class *Cephalopoda,* called *Sepia,* or Cuttle-fish. But before we go any further, let us inquire what is meant by a *Cephalopod.* Our readers have already learned that *Gasteropod* means stomach and foot, and that *acephalous* means headless; now here we have a word which takes a portion of each of the others (*cephal*—head, and *peda,* or *poda*—a foot), consequently *ceph-a-lo-po-da* is a class of molluscous animals which have their feet, or organs of motion, arranged round the head, something, you may suppose, like the celebrated hero of nursery rhymes,

"Tom Toddy, all head and no body."

Only our bag-shaped Mr. Sepia, with his great,

round, staring eyes, and numerous legs or arms, whichever you please to call them, all twisting and twining about like so many serpents, is a much more formidable-looking individual. A strange fellow is this altogether; he has a shell, but he does not use it for a covering, he carries it inside of him, and it serves the purpose of a sort of backbone. It is horny and calcareous, light and porous, as our readers well know, having most likely often used it to take out unsightly blots, or erase mistakes in their copy or cyphering books.

When Mr. Sepia walks abroad, he sticks his little round body upright, so that his eyes and mouth, which is armed with a parrot-like beak, are brought close to the surface over which he passes, while his long twining legs go sprawling about in all directions. On the insides of these legs are a great number of small circular suckers, by means of which the animal can fix itself to any object so tightly, that it is almost impossible to detach it without tearing off part of the limb. Woe be to the poor unfortunate fish that chances to come in its way; the snaky arms are thrown around it, and made fast, and away goes the cephalopod for a ride, eating on the road to lose no time, on the finny steed that carries it. In some species each of the suckers has a hook in the centre, which, of course, renders the hold yet firmer, and, no doubt, adds to the disagreeable sensation which their tight compression must cause. It is likely that these hooks are intended to retain the hold of soft and slippery prey, which might otherwise be too agile for the " ugly customer," that would affectionately embrace it. But Mr. Sepia, though well armed in front, is rather open to attacks in the rear of his soft naked body. To provide for such an emergency, he is furnished with a little bag of inky fluid, which he squirts out in the face of his pursuer, and escapes under cover of the cloud. This is the substance used by painters, and called sepia, whence the generic name of the mollusks which produce it.

In the British seas none of these cephalopods attain so large a size as to be formidable to man, as they do in warmer climates. It was asserted by Dens, an old navigator, that in the African seas, while three of his men were employed during a calm in scraping the sides of the vessel, they were attacked by a monstrous Cuttle-fish, which seized them in its arms, and drew two of them under water, the third man was with difficulty rescued by cutting off one of the creature's limbs, which was as thick at the base as the foreyard of the ship, and had suckers as large as ladles ; the rescued sailor was so horrified by the monster that he died delirious a few hours after. An account is also given of another crew who were similarly attacked off the coast of Angola; the creature threw its arms across the vessel, and had nearly succeeded in dragging it down, and was only prevented doing so by the severing of its limbs with swords and hatchets. A diligent observer of nature has asserted that in the Indian seas Cuttle-fish are often seen two fathoms broad across the centre, with arms nine fathoms long. Only think, what a monster ! with a body twelve feet across, and eight or ten legs like water-snakes, some six-and-thirty feet long. Well may it be said, that the Indians when they go out in boats are in dread of such, and never sail without an axe for their protection.

There is a story told by a gentleman named Beale, who, while searching for shells upon the rocks of the Bonin Islands, encountered a species of Cuttle-fish called by the whalers "the Rock-squid," and rashly endeavoured to secure it. This cephalopod, whose body was not bigger than a large clenched hand, had tentacles at least four feet across, and having its retreat to the sea cut off by

Mr. Beale, twined its limbs around that gentleman's arm, which was bared to the shoulder for the
purpose of thrusting into holes of the rocks after
shells, and endeavoured to get its horny beak in a
position for biting. The narrator describes the
sickening sensation of horror which chilled his very
blood, as he felt the creature's cold slimy grasp,
and saw its large staring eyes fixed on him, and the
beak opening and closing. He called loudly for
help, and was soon joined by his companion, who
relieved him by destroying the Cuttle-fish with a
knife, and detaching the limbs piece by piece.

There are several species of these cephalopods;
the most generally distributed appears to be the

O. VULGARIS.          S. VULGARIS.          S. OFFICINALIS.

*Octopus vulgaris,* or Common Cuttle-fish, which is

scmetimes found on our own shores, where also may
be obtained the Common Sepiola, *S. vulgaris*,
usually about three inches long, and the Officinal
Cuttle-fish, *S. officinalis*, which is about a foot in
length ; we give below small figures of each of these
three species, to show the difference in the shape :
the two last, it will be observed, have, in addition
to the eight tentacles, which give the generic
name *Octopus*, signifying eight, two long side arms,
the use of which does not appear to be very clearly
determined.

---

## NAUTILUS AND AMMONITE.

The Nautili are called testaceous cephalopods;
our readers know, or ought to know, the meaning
of both these terms.  Like the Cuttle-fish, they are
sometimes called *Polypi*, because they have many
arms or tentacles, the word *poly*, with which a great
number of English words commence, being the
Greek for many.  An ancient writer named Aris-
totle, after describing the naked cephalopods, says,
" There are also two polypi in shells; one is called
by some, *nautilus*, and by others, *nauticus*.  It is
like the polypus, but its shell resembles a hollow

comb or pecten, and is not attached. This polypus ordinarily feeds near the sea-shore; sometimes it is thrown by the waves on the dry land, and the shell falling from it, is caught, and there dies. The other is in a shell like a snail, and this does not go out of its shell, but remains in it like a snail, and sometimes stretches forth its *cirrhi.*" The first of these animals, there can be no doubt, is the Argonaut, or Paper Nautilus, and the latter that which is called the True Nautilus, of both of which species let us say a few words, which we will introduce by quoting some beautiful lines from a poem called " The Pelican Island," by James Montgomery :—

> " Light as a flake of foam upon the wind,
>   Keel upwards from the deep, emerged a shell,
>   Shaped like the moon ere half her orb is filled:
>   Fraught with young life it righted as it rose,
>   And moved at will along the yielding water.
>   The native pilot of this little bark
>   Put out a tier of oars on either side;
>   Spread to the wafted breeze a two-fold sail,
>   And mounted up and glided down the billow,
>   In happy freedom, pleased to fill the air,
>   And wander in the luxury of light."

The tiny mariner here alluded to is the Paper Nautilus, common in the Mediterranean and some

tropical seas; its scientific name is *Argonauta argo.*
In the mythology, we read that *Argo* was the name
of a ship that carried a certain Grecian named
Jason, and a crew of *argives,* in search of adventures. Some say that the term is derived from a
Greek word signifying swift. This party of mari-
ners, said to be the first that ever sailed upon the
sea, was called *Argonauts,* or, as it might be freely
translated, seamen of the ship Argo. *Nauticus,* in
Latin, signifies anything relating to ships or navigation, and here you have the whole origin of the
name of this little Argonaut, about which we must
sing you a song written by Mary Howitt before we
proceed further :—

" Who was the first sailor? tell me who can;
　　Old father Neptune!—no, you're wrong,
　There was another ere Neptune began;
　　Who was he? tell me. Tightly and strong,
　　　Over the waters he went—he went,
　　　Over the waters he went!

" Who was the first sailor? tell me who can;
　　Old father Noah!—no, you're wrong,
　There was another ere Noah began,
　　Who was he? tell me. Tightly and strong,
　　　Over the waters he went—he went,
　　　Over the waters he went.

' Who was the first sailor? tell me who can;
 Old father Jason!—no, you're wrong,
There was another ere Jason began,
 Don't be a blockhead, boy! Tightly and strong,
  Over the waters he went—he went,
  Over the waters he went.


" Ha! 'tis nought but the poor little Nautilus—
 Sailing away in his pearly shell;
He has no need of a compass like us,
 Foul or fair weather he manages well!
  Over the water he goes—he goes,
  Over the water he goes."


Many more poems of the like nature we might quote, for this little shelled cephalopod has been a favourite with the poets time out of mind, and in some instances they and the less imaginative naturalists have disagreed in their accounts of its form and operations; for instance, Pope says—

" Learn of the little Nautilus to sail,
 Spread the thin oar and catch the driving gale."


" Catch a fiddle-stick," say some naturalists, the little Nautilus does nothing of the sort; and if you go to him to learn navigation, you will never be much of a sailor. He may teach you how to sink to the bottom and rise again, and that kind of knowledge might be worth something to you if you could breathe under water; and he might teach you how to swim, but not how to sail, for, in spite of all poetic theories, he does the former and not the latter. Most usually he walks about at the bottom of the sea on his long arms, something like the Cuttle-fish, feeding on the marine vegetation; the shell is then uppermost. If we could look inside of it we should see numerous little chambers or cells, the larger and outermost of which only are inhabited by the mollusk, the others being filled with air render the whole light and buoyant. Through the centre of these chambers, down to the smallest of them, runs a membranous tube which can be exhausted or filled with fluid at the pleasure of the animal, and the difference thus effected in the weight of the shell enables it to sink or swim; in the latter case, up it goes to the surface, and "keel upwards from the deep," emerges, as the poet has said, but once there it soon reverses its position. The shell becomes like a boat it is true, but its inhabitant neither points a sail nor plies the oar, but propels itself along stem foremost by a muscular action, which by alternately compressing and loosening a kind of siphon, throws out jets or gushes of water, which, by the resistance they meet with from the surrounding fluid, give the desired onward motion, and away the swimmer goes, his long arms gathered closely together, and streaming behind like the tail of a comet, and its round eyes keeping a sharp look-out on either side. Should it espy danger, the body and limbs are withdrawn into the shell, and the fluid driven through the central tube, so as to compress the air in the pearly cells, and down sinks the swimmer once again to his native depths, where

> "The floor is of sand like the mountain drift,
>    And the pearl shells spangle the flinty snow;
> And from coral rocks the sea-plants lift
>    Their boughs where the tides and billows flow.
>    The water is calm and still below,
> For the winds and waves are absent there;
>    And the sands are bright as the stars that glow
> In the motionless fields of upper air.
> And life in rare and beautiful forms
>    Is sporting amid those bowers of stone,
> And is safe, when the wrathful spirit of storms
>    Has made the top of the waves his own."

On the following page we give two figures of the Argonaut, one of which represents him crawling at the bottom of the sea, and the other swimming on the surface.

The True, or Pearly Nautilus (*N. Pompilius*),
the origin of whose specific name we have been
unable to discover, is much like the Argonaut in
appearance and general construction; the shell is
externally smoother and more iridescent, it is also
generally somewhat thicker than the former kind,
and has internally more chambers or divisions; its
pearly lustre renders it a beautiful ornament, and
the large size it frequently attains a very con-

spicuous one.   Its inhabitant has several peculiarities of organization, which distinguish it from
the Argonauts, but into these we need not enter;
neither can we pause to describe the other species
of Nautili, the shells of which, like those of the
Cowry and other univalves, are covered with a
membrane which hides their beauty.   This membrane or mantle sometimes extends some distance
beyond the edge of the shell, and, being of a light
and filmy appearance, may have been mistaken for
a sail hoisted by the creature to catch the breeze,

while its long arms, thrust up into the air or down
into the water, may have been thought to be masts
or oars, so that the poets are not so much to be
blamed, if they say as Wordsworth does—

"Spread, tiny Nautilus, the living sail
    Dive at thy choice, or catch the freshening gale."

Nearly allied to the Nautili are these beautiful
fossil shells called Ammonites, from their fancied
resemblance to the horns of a heathen deity or god,
called Jupiter Ammon. These shells, at once the
wonder and pride of geologists, are found in the
chalk formations, and thousands of years must have
passed away since they were inhabited by living
creatures. The Nautili which swam and sported
with them at the depths of the ocean, as is proved
by the shells of many species found in the same
chalky deposits, have still their living represen-
tatives; but those winding galleries and pearly
chambers once fragile as paper and brittle as glass,
now turned into, and surrounded by solid stone
are all shells of extinct species, and we can hardly
see and handle them without some degree of awe
and reverence; when we reflect on the great and
wonderful changes that have passed over the earth
since they were formed by a hand Divine, instinct

with the breath of life, and then to be embedded in
the rock as everlasting characters by which the
unborn generations of men might read in history
of those changes, and of the providential dealings
of God with his creatures. Of these Ammonites,
and other fossil shells, much more will have to be
said in our proposed geological volume; the poem
which follows will very appropriately conclude the
above remarks, and our present little work on

NAUTILUS.                    AMMONITE.

shells—beautiful, wonderful shells! useful, ornamental, instructive! The subject is one which we
would earnestly invite our young readers to study:
it is but here introduced; we have picked up a few,
very few, of the wonders and beauties of conchology, and presented them to their notice in the
hope that they may be induced to desire a more
intimate acquaintance with this branch of natural

science, which has been hitherto greatly neglected. To understand it thoroughly, much attention and perseverance will be required, but even a slight acquaintance with it will yield both pleasure and profit to the mind.

# THE NAUTILUS AND THE AMMONITE.

The Nautilus and the Ammonite,
  Were launched in storm and strife;
Each sent to float in its tiny boat,
  On the wide, wild sea of life.

And each could swim on the ocean's brim,
  And anon its sails could furl,
And sink to sleep in the great sea deep,
  In a palace all of pearl.

And theirs was a bliss more fair than this,
  That we feel in our colder time;
For they were rife in a tropic life
  In a brighter, happier clime.

They swam 'mid isles whose summer smiles
  No wintry winds annoy;
Whose groves were palm, whose air was balm,
  Whose life was only joy.

They roam'd all day through creek and bay,
  And travers'd the ocean deep;
And at night they sank on a coral bank,
  In its fairy bowers to sleep.

And the monsters vast of ages past,
  They beheld in their ocean caves;
And saw them ride in their power and pride,
  And sink in their billowy graves.

Thus hand in hand, from strand to strand,
　They sail'd in mirth and glee;
Those fairy shells, with their crystal cells,
　Twin creatures of the sea.

But they came at last to a sea long past,
　And as they reach'd its shore,
The Almighty's breath spake out in death,
　And the Ammonite liv'd no more.

And the Nautilus now in its shelly prow,
　As o'er the deep it strays,
Still seems to seek, in bay and creek,
　Its companion of other days.

And thus do we, in life's stormy sea,
　As we roam from shore to shore;
While tempest-tost, seek the lov'd —the lost,
　But find them on earth no more!

　　　　　　　　　G. F. RICHARDSON.

# SHELLS OF COMMON OCCURRENCE.

## BY WILLIAM WALLACE FYFE.

———

THE *Limacidæ*, or land-slugs, are represented con-chologically by the thin crustaceous shells found on dissection within their mantles, being, as every-body familiarly knows, outwardly destitute of shell. This shield is protective of the cavity employed in respiration. Figs. 1, 2, 3, and 4 represent four of these shields, extracted from the milky, yellow, tree, and spotted slugs respectively (*Limax agrestis, L. flavus, L. arborum, L. cinereus*).

These creatures, as every lover of a garden too well knows, are powerful vegetable feeders, making their appearance in damp weather in multitudes like an Egyptian plague. Their destructive voracity enables them to secrete an exuberance of white milky mucilage from their bodies, to discharge this copiously when irritated, and to mark their devour-ing tracks in their slime. Like linseed and other mucilaginous matter, animal and vegetable, slugs, when boiled, have been employed as a cure for consumption. When hard pressed by hunger only will they eat dead earth-worms, and hence their blight falls chiefly on the growing plant. The observer may occasionally have felt startled to see the *Limax* suspended by an almost invisible but very tenacious thread which it possesses the power of spinning, betwixt him and the light. This is

1. 2. 3. 4.

1. Limax agrestis (the Milky Slug), *Müller.* 2. L. flavus (the Yellow Slug), *Linnæus.* 3. L. arborum (the Tree Slug), *Chautereaux.* 4. L. cinereus (the Spotted Slug), *Müller.*

used by the slug to drop from on high. Like the spider, it exudes this mucous thread from the secretions of its body. Encumbered with no mansion which it must carry on its back like the snail (*Helix*), the slug is yet more hardy without its shelter than the *Helix*, and remains active far into the winter, when the other lies dormant in the crevice of the wall.

The most common slug of the fields, *L. agrestis,* or milky slug, about an inch and a half long, is the most destructive of molluscous animals, devouring the roots of plants as well as their leaves. It is bisexual and very prolific, breeding several times a year; and Chautereaux counted three hundred and eighty eggs deposited by two individuals betwixt April and November, laying from thirty to seventy at a time. They rapidly increase in size, and reach maturity in three months, although they probably begin to lay eggs in about two. The *L. flavus*, or *variegatus* (for although the lower surface be yellowish-grey, the upper is thickly and irregularly-spotted blackish brown), has a limpid slime, but secretes, when irritated, a thicker bluish-white mucus. On reaching any twig or place where there occurs a difficulty of proceeding, it allows itself to drop or be slowly lowered by its thread of adhesive mucus, which at length gives way. This is the slug which is found under damp turf and stones, beside walls and among plants. It is twice the size of the field slug, being from three to four and sometimes even five inches long. Mr. E. J. Lowe says it is best known as the cellar slug, and is in such situations gregarious. The tree slug (*L. arborum*) is greyish, with marbled side-stripes, and a dusky band along the back. It feeds upon wood and affects decaying trees, whence it uses its mucous thread to descend. The spotted grey slug (*L. cinereus*), best known as the black slug, but not to be confounded with the *Arion,* though less common than the field slug, is very abundant in damp situations, under decaying wood and fragments of stones in gardens, hedges, etc., and in cellars and outhouses; copious rain, or even dew, enticing it from its retreat. It is the largest of the slug family, being six inches long, and will be found handsomely formed when attentively surveyed. It is circular on the back, acute and pointed at the tail; with upper tentacles of great length and short lower ones; it secretes colourless mucus. The shield is slightly stained with pink. It deposits during spring from fifty to sixty eggs, attached in heaps together, under stones and at the roots of grass and trunks of trees.

The *Helix,* or snail, has a shell spirally rolled, and although possessing no operculum, it substitutes that filmy mucous covering, by means of which it closes up its shell, and which is perforated with holes to enable it to breathe. Remaining concealed in obscurity during the day, it comes forth to feed evening and morning, or after rain, retiring from business altogether in the winter into a hole or crevice, or amongst moss, and shutting up shop till the return of solar heat. When in motion it carries its shell balanced obliquely on its back, and keeps advancing and retracting its tentacles. It is quite as destructive to vegetation as the slug.

We should have enough to do to describe all the species and varieties, for of Helices alone we

5-6.                                          7-8.

9-10.                   11-12.                13-14.

5-6. Vitrina pellucida (the Transparent Glass Bubble Shell), *Müller.* 7-8. Zonites cellarius (the Cellar Snail), *ibid.* 9-10. Z. alliarius (the Garlic Snail), *ibid.* 11-12. Z. nitidulus (the Dull Snail), *Draparnaud.* 13-14. Z. purus (the Delicate Snail), *Alder.*

may count at least forty. The *Vitrina pellucida,* or transparent glassy snail (Figs. 5 and 6), found among the putrescent leaves, moss, and decaying wood of plantations and hedge-bottoms, and also under stones, is an exceedingly thin, transparent, glossy, smooth, and fragile watery-green shell, through which the mantle of the animal within is reflected. It is elliptical in form, with three and a

half depressed whorls. The shell of the *Zonites cellarius*, a cellar snail (Figs. 7 and 8), is also shining, smooth, and pellucid, and of a pale yellowish horn-colour. It is found in cellars, drains, and shady courts, in fields and woods, under stones, and amongst grass. The shell of the garlic snail (*Zonites alliarius*, Figs. 9 and 10), is nearly flat, and more convex, yellower in colour, but equally pellucid, smooth, polished, and fragile. Some of these creatures have, when alive, a strong odour of garlic, some have it on being plunged in hot water (which is the readiest way of killing them for the shell), though not when alive. Its .numbers in our bag, as swept down a river, are somewhat extraordinary.

The little *Zonites nitidulus* (Figs. 11 and 12), takes from its shell the name of little shining snail. A deep umbilicus is seen in the shell. The animal is also called the " dull snail," from its leaden colour; but the shell, three-tenths of an inch in diameter, is of a yellowish horn-colour, and very like *Z. cellarius*. Another of these small shells, tho delicate snail, *Z. purus* (Figs. 13 and 14), is only two lines or less in diameter ; it is not very common, but, like the rest, smooth, glossy, and transparent, and may be known by its mouth,

which is placed obliquely. It cannot well be confounded with *Z. radiatus*, the rayed snail shell (Figs. 15 and 16), for that, although polished, shining, and pellucid, is regularly striated or wrinkled, and is horn or amber coloured, and two lines in diameter. *Z. excavatus* (Figs. 17 and 18) is a quarter of an inch shell, of which there are multitudes in our bag, found under felled timber

15-16.        17-18.

19-20.        21-22.

15-16. Z. radiatus (the Rayed Snail), *Alder.* 17-18. Z. excavatus (the Excavated Snail), *Bean.* 19-20. Z. nitidus (the Shining Snail), *Müller.* 21-22. Z. crystallinus (the Crystalline Snail), *ibid.*

and decayed wood. *Z. nitidus*, the shining snail (Figs. 19 and 20) is likewise pellucid, the colour being brownish horn, its diameter a quarter of an inch. In pine-beds and damp hothouses, where it is found largely congregated, sad havoc is perpetrated by this tiny snail. The *Z. crystallinus* of Müller (Figs. 21 and 22) scarcely exceeds an eighth of an inch in diameter, and occurs amongst decayed leaves and stones.

Of the Helices proper, we figure fifteen different species; they are mostly too well known to require to be more than mentioned. Of these the largest and most familiar, *Helix aspersa,* or common snail (Fig. 23), is the largest and most destructive in the

23.      24-25.

26-27.

3. Helix aspersa (the Common Snail), *Müller.* 24-25. H. revelata (the Green Snail), *Férussac.* 26-27. H. nemoralis (the Girdled Snail), *Linnæus.*

garden. Its usual diameter is an inch and a-half. It is olive coloured, with dark brown bands. The shell is in reality not slimy, though apparently rough on the surface. It is alleged that barrels are exported as a dainty to America, and that the London markets are largely supplied with it as a remedy for pulmonary complaints. In the United States it has been successfully acclimatized, and is now

getting common. It has a penchant for nettles,
wild celery, elder *Primula vulgaris*, and will climb
walls, and apple and scented poplar trees, to a great
height, but is capable of a long fast. Mr. Lowe
mentions one that fasted one hundred and eight
days in summer. The green snail (*H. revelata*,
Figs. 24 and 25) is very rare and pretty. It was
added by Edward Forbes in 1839; he found it near
Doyle's monument in Guernsey. The yellowish-
green *H. nemoralis*, or girdled snail (Figs. 26 and
27), is abundant and beautiful, and known to every

28-29.

30-31.

28-29. H. hortensis (the Garden Snail), *Montagu.*   30-31.
H. arbustorum (the Shrub Snail), *Linnæus.*

one. This snail also has been introduced into
North America, where it is becoming common. It
is about seven-eighths of an inch in diameter. In

about an hour after a shower, the banks they frequent become quite covered over with them, where in dry weather not one is to be found, as they retire into holes in the ground, and amongst grass, roots, and rubbish. The *H. hortensis,* garden snail (Figs. 28 and 29), is, like the preceding, very varied in its colours, though less in its size, which is three-fourths of an inch in diameter. The shrub snail (Figs. 30 and 31), which nearly resembles this, is pretty and interesting. The zoned snail *H. virgata* (Figs. 32 and 33), is more peculiar to

32-33.          34-35.

36-37.          38-39.

32-33. H. virgata (the Zoned Snail), *Da Costa.* 34-35. H. caperata (the Black-tipped Snail), *Montagu.* 36-37. H. ericetorum (the Heath Snail), *Müller.* 38-39. H. hispida (the Bristly Snail), *Linnæus.*

chalk and lime districts; and the little black-tipped snail, *H. caperata* (Figs. 34 and 35), which might at first sight be mistaken for the zoned snail, is a

Dorsetshire snail, added by Dr. Pulteney.  Of the
others which are figured, the heath snail is pale
green in colour, and the bristly snail (*II. hispida*),
which associates with it on the dry heath, is nearly
greyish.  The last shell is scattered over with
bristles, but its diameter is only a quarter of an
inch.  The prickly snail (Fig. 42), though more

40-41.        42.        43-44.

45-46.        47-48.        49-50.

40-41. H. sericea, *Draparnaud*.  42. II. aculeata (the
Prickly Snail), *Müller*.  43-44. H. fulva (the Top-shaped
Snail.  45-46. II. pulchella (the White Snail), *Müller*.
47-48. H. rotundata (the Radiated Snail), *ibid.* 49-50. H.
pygmœa (the Pigmy Snail), *Draparnaud* (much exagge-
rated, see scale betwixt).

minute, is still more remarkable from having the
appearance of large prickles on its shell.  Amongst
these very small shells are the top-shaped and white
snail, the radiated, and finally the pigmy snail,
whose diameter is less than a line.

We shall still go to our bag for one more hand-
ful of miscellaneous shells, which differ much from

the Helices now disposed of so far as we have got them in our budget. Our greatest regret is the absence of *H. pomatia*, the largest of the British land shells, the favourite shell food of the Romans, still eaten in many parts of modern Europe.

The *Bulimus obscurus*, dull or dusky twist shell, is considered to derive its first or generic name from a Greek term signifying insatiable hunger (βούλιμος), and its specific from the Latin, indicative of its colour (dusky or dull), for scientific jargon is generally macaronic, and by no means minds a Babel of languages. The shell is not large, being generally under half an inch in length and a couple of lines in breadth. It is unpolished in appearance; and though the animal within bears a resemblance to the Helices, or snails, the shell without tapers much more considerably, and in crawling the creature carries its shelter balanced on its back, directed a little to the right, at an angle of 50°, or drags it along the ground, and holds it when at rest at an angle of 45°. It is found in woods and under mossy trees, on walls and under stones. It crawls with speed, as if to justify the imputation of being very devouring, and of getting rapidly through its fortune. It is by no means rare in England. Macgillivray and Duncan first found it in Scotland amidst the ruins of Dunottar Castle; and it must have an affinity for old castles, as Mr. E. J. Lowe mentions as a Midland habitat Nottingham Castle yard.    Three examples next turn up of the chrysalis snail shell, or pupa.    Their fancied resemblance to chrysalids give the pupæ their name.    They are similar in their habits to the *Bulimi*, feeding on vegetable substances; residing under mosses, herbage, or stones; inert in continued drought, and searching mostly for food at night, when the grass is moist.    Unlike the *Bulimus*, however, the *Pupa umbilicata*, for instance, is a slow mover, and carries its shell at the moderate inclination of 15°; and the shell, instead of tapering like the *Bulimus*, comes abruptly to an

51.          52.          53.          54.

51. Bulimus obscurus (the Dusky Twist Shell), *Müller*, 52. Pupa umbilicata (the Umbilicated Chrysalis Shell), *Draparnaud*. 53. Pupa pygmœa (the Pigmy Chrysalis Shell). 54. P. substriata (the Six-toothed Chrysalis Shell), *Jeffreys*.

apex.    It is very minute, usually only the ninth of an inch long and the twentieth of an inch broad.

Wherever limestone or chalk abound, there it is found, whether in the cracks of old walls, amidst ivy, under stones and the bark of trees, or on the sea-cliffs and valleys. If, however, the *P. umbilicata* be minute, the *P. pygmœa* is exceedingly minute, being not more than a line in length. By most authors this tiny shell, found, though not abundantly, in all parts of Great Britain and Ireland, both in wet and dry situations, but principally in dry, is classed as *Vertigo pygmœa.* The *P. substriata,* so called from its cylindrical, shining, polished little surface being streaked longitudinally, is much the same size, a line long, half a line broad, and though rare where it is found, is at the same time widely diffused from Cornwall, Devonshire, and Suffolk, to Preston, Lancaster, and Newcastle-upon-Tyne. And speaking of Newcastle-upon-Tyne, it ought to be mentioned that Mr. Joshua Alder, the great molluscous authority and *genius loci,* has pointed out a remarkable structure in the interior of the *pupa,* the use of which has not yet been ascertained. It consists of a raised thread-like laminar process, winding spirally round the columella, and similar lamina running spirally on the upper side of the volutes, with small flat transverse plaits at intervals in the interior.

The widely-spread *Balea fragilis* has been confounded with the *pupæ*, but it is far too tapering. It is a small, thin, delicate, shining, and rather transparent shell, of a yellowish horn-colour, and in length about the third of an inch. It is found in trunks of trees, and amidst mosses and lichens. The dark close shell, *Clausilia nigricans*, with

55.                    56.

55. Balea fragilis (the Fragile Moss Shell), *Draparnaud.*
56. Clausilia nigricans (the Dark Close Shell), *various.*

which we have grouped it, is better known as the common *Clausilia*; but it is quite a conchologist's shell, having long escaped vulgar popularity, though very generally distributed throughout Great Britain. This exclusiveness is due to its habits and colour, which render it far from easy of detection. Its length is half an inch, breadth from a twelfth to an eighth, and it inhabits old walls. The animal, as may be inferred from the shell, is very thin and slender, so much so that in motion it is incapable of raising its shell, but drags it along in the same line as its foot and neck, although when going to

repose it inclines it at an angle of 70 . It derives
its generic name from a shelly bone attached to

57                    58-59.

57. Zua lubrica (the Common Varnished Shell), *Müller.*
    58-59. Azeca tridens (the Glossy Trident Shell), *Pulteney.*

the columellar teeth, and termed the *clausium*, from
closing up the aperture when the animal has
retired within its habitation. The next little group,
*Zua lubrica* (common varnished shell), and *Azeca
tridens* (glossy trident shell), are parallel in character,
only the *Zua* is toothless, the *Azeca* ovate and
toothed in the mouth. Both inhabit close shady
wood, moss, and under stones and decayed leaves.
The one is not quite, the other about, a quarter of
an inch in length. The next group comprises the
needle agate shell (*Achatina acicula*), the shell of
the common amber snail (*Succinea putris*), and two
*Physæ* or bubble shells (*P. fontinalis* and *P. hypnorum*). The first is indeed minute, interesting, and
extremely delicate, having six convolutions, though
only a fifth of an inch in length; but, indeed, dead
specimens found in old Saxon coffins are more
frequent than living ones occurring amongst roots
of grass and moss. *Succinea* is from *succinum,*

amber, and *putris* means filthy; but there is nothing repulsive about the shell, which, with its variety, *S. gracilis* (slender, is found always near water,

60.          61-62.          63.          64.

60. Achatina acicula (the Needle Agate Shell), *Müller.*
    61-62. Succinea putris (the Common Amber Snail),
    *Linnæus.*  63. Physa fontinalis (the Stream Bubble
    Shell), *ibid.* 64. P. hypnorum (the Slender Bubble Shell),
    *ibid.*

either crawling on mud or damp, or attached to succulent plants. They are never found, however, in the water. Not so *Physa fontinalis*, as its name implies, *physa* (φυσαῶ), inflated or blown out, and *fontinalis*, residing in springs or fountains. Yet the creature is herbivorous, feeding on the leaves, especially of *Potamogeton*, in lakes and rivers. Beneath the water it glides along with moderate, uniform motion, produced by the undulations of its foot. In the air it advances by jerks, without protruding its tentacula: and Montagu asserts that it will sometimes let itself down gradually by a thread affixed to the surface of the water, as the *Limax* drops itself from the branch of a tree. *P. hypnorum* is found in ditches and stagnant pools in many parts

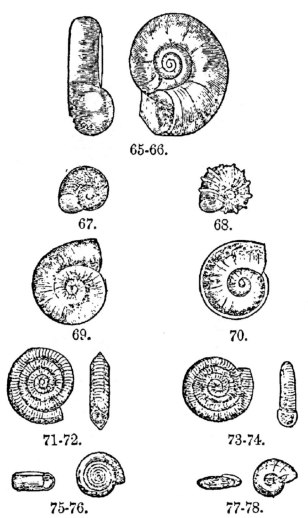

65-66.

67.  68.

69.  70.

71-72.  73-74.

75-76.  77-78.

65-66. Planorbis corneus (the Horny Coil Shell), *Linnæus.*
67. P. albus (the White Coil Shell), *Müller.*  68. P.
nautileus (the Nautilus Coil Shell), *Linnæus.*  69. P.
marginatus (the Margined Coil Shell), *Draparnaud.*  70.
P. carinatus (the Carinated Coil Shell), *Müller.*  71-72.
P. vortex (the Whorl Coil Shell), *Linnæus.*  73-74. P.
spirorbis (the Rolled Coil Shell), *Müller.*  75-76. P. contortus (the Twisted Coil Shell), *Linnæus.*  77-78. P.
nitidus (the Fountain Coil Shell), *ibid.*

of Great Britain and Ireland.   The mud is prolific
of shells; witness the Planorbis family, of which

79.        80.                        81.

82.        83.        84-85.        86.

79. Limnæus auricularius (the Wide-eared Mud Shell),
*Linnæus.*    80. L. pereger (the Travelled Mud Shell),
*Müller.*   81. L. stagnalis (the Lake Mud Shell), *Linnæus.*
82. L. fossarius (the Ditch Mud Shell), *Turton.*   83. L.
glaber (the Eight-Whorled Mud Shell), *ibid.*   84-85. L.
palustris (the Marsh Mud Shell), *Linnæus.*   86. L. gluti-
nosus (the Glutinous Mud Shell), *Müller.*

nine species are here figured.   They have been
likened to the fossil Ammonites, for which they might
be taken as miniature copies.   The name is hence
a kind of contradiction in terms, compounded of
the words which signify "flat" and "ball."   The
largest is the *P. corneus* (Figs. 65 and 66), an inch
in diameter; the others are *P. albus,* from one-

fourth to one-fifth; *P. nautilcus,* one-eighth to one-tenth; *P. marginatus,* five-eighths; *P. carinatus, P. spirorbis,* one-fourth; and *P. contortus,* one-fifth of an inch in diameter, respectively; whilst *P. vortex* is usually only from three to four lines, and *P. nitidus* two and a-half lines. These shells are found in the slow rivers, pools, and stagnant waters of England. The *P. vortex* does not actually reside in the mud, but on its surface; but more especially occupies the stems and leaves of plants, both in and out of the water, retiring into recesses and cavities in the banks formed by the plants or their overlying stems or leaves. In point of fact, the mud shells, *par excellence,* are the group of *Limnæcea,* of which there are given seven examples (Figs. 79—86). The family is wide-spread, the shells are fragile; and Mr. Lowe has noticed that the property of walking upside down on the ceiling, appertaining to the house-fly (*Musca domestica*), has been introduced by the Limnæus into the watery regions, " for it as easily crawls upside down on the surface of the water basking in the sun, as it moves in the ordinary manner on the surface of the mud." The lake and river limpets, *Ancylus oblongus* and *A. fluviatilis* (Figs. 87 and 88) are small breathing animals; and the minute sedge

shell, *Carychium minimum* (Fig. 89), though common, is almost microscopical.

The embryo naturalist, perchance, may imagine
that a complete cabinet of common shells could be
easily set up; but it is not every one whose enthu-

87.        88.        89.                    90.

87. Ancylus fluviatilis (the Common River Limpet), *Müller.*
88. A. oblongus (the Oblong Lake Limpet), *Kightfoot,*
89. Carychium minimum (the Minute Sedge Shell),
*Müller.*   90. Limax brunneus (the Brown Slug), var.,
*Draparnaud.*

siasm would lead them to undergo the task. The
man of science is well aware that he must trace out
the wonders of the living creation in their native
haunts, in order .to their perfect comprehension;
we are therefore glad to know that the York
Natural History Society collects and sends out to
subscribers the shells and fossils of different British
districts and strata, at something like ten shillings
a set.

THE END.

Lightning Source UK Ltd.
Milton Keynes UK
UKOW03n0136021214

242497UK00011B/251/P